# How To Restore and Customize **Auto Upholstery & Interiors**

# How To Restore and Customize **Auto Upholstery & Interiors**

*Dennis W. Parks*

**MOTORBOOKS**

To my wife, Sandy, for all her patience, support, and understanding as I try to make a buck
to support my hot rod habit.

First published in 2005 by Motorbooks, an imprint of MBI Publishing Company, Galtier Plaza, Suite 200, 380 Jackson Street, St. Paul, MN 55101-3885 USA

The information in this book is true and complete to the best of our knowledge. All recommendations are made without any guarantee on the part of the author or Publisher, who also disclaim any liability incurred in connection with the use of this data or specific details.

This publication has been prepared solely by MBI Publishing Company and is not approved or licensed by any other entity. We recognize that some words, model names, and designations mentioned herein are the property of the trademark holder. We use them for identification purposes only. This is not an official publication.

Motorbooks titles are also available at discounts in bulk quantity for industrial or sales-promotional use. For details write to Special Sales Manager at MBI Publishing Company, Galtier Plaza, Suite 200, 380 Jackson Street, St. Paul, MN 55101-3885 USA.

Library of Congress Cataloging-in-Publication
     Parks, Dennis, 1959–
         How to restore and customize auto upholstery and
     interiors / by Dennis W. Parks.
         p. cm. -- (Motorbooks workshop)
     ISBN-13: 978-0-7603-2043-3
     ISBN-10: 0-7603- 2043-8
         1. Automobiles--Upholstery--Maintenance and repair.
         2. Automobiles--Interiors--Maintenance and repair.
         3. Automobiles--Customizing. I. Title. II. Series.

TL255.2.P364 2005
629.2'77--dc2

Editor: Kris Palmer and Peter Bodensteiner
Designer: Chris Fayers

Printed in China

**On the front cover, main:** The 1932 Ford Phaeton is a true classic, whether restored or modified. Providing seating for four, it also provides "open air cruising" with the top down, or can keep the passengers and driver out of the weather with the top up and the optional side curtains installed. This particular Deuce belongs to Randy Bergfeld and looks as good with the top up as it does down. A neutral color leather interior in a traditional pattern allows for a multitude of paint schemes if Randy should ever decide to repaint the car. Thank you for your time, Randy. **Inset:** Upholsterer Don Albers builds the seat bottom cushion for a reproduction Cobra.

**On the back cover:** Use a well-worn putty knife to push headliner material up behind the serrated strips that hold up the edges.

*About the author:*
Dennis W. Parks began his professional publishing career as a freelance magazine photographer/writer in 1985. His work has been seen in more than 165 articles in *Street Rodder, Rod & Custom, Hot Rod, Rodder's Digest, Super Chevy,* and *Custom Classic Trucks,* as well as several other publications. *How To Restore and Customize Auto Upholstery and Interiors* is the fifth book that Dennis has written for MBI. Two of his books, *How To Build A Hot Rod* and *How To Paint Your Car* are among MBI's best sellers. Currently employed by a major contractor for the defense industry, Dennis has worked as a technical writer for the last seven years. He lives with his wife in a St. Louis, Missouri suburb. While not working on a book project, Dennis enjoys traveling, building hot rods, and woodworking.

# CONTENTS

# ACKNOWLEDGMENTS

I must thank Don Albers, Jack Waller, and Nick Mayden for their assistance and hospitality in allowing me to photograph them while they did their magic. Without them opening their shops to me, the how-to photo sequences would have been impossible.

Thank you to Joan Thornton at E&J Upholstery, Shawn Appleman at Appleman Interiors, and Sam Wright at Sam Wright Hot Rod Interiors for reading through the book and providing invaluable information. Thanks also go to the various companies that provided additional photos and information.

Wishing you the best in your upholstery project,

—Dennis W. Parks

# INTRODUCTION

Automotive upholstery has a great impact on the overall appearance of a vehicle and has a definite influence on your desire to ride in that vehicle. If you need to get from point A to point B, other than getting there safely and on time, your main concern is that you are comfortable while in transit.

What we perceive as comfortable varies from person to person and sometimes from trip to trip. If you are making a solo banzai run across country, comfort may mean room for a cooler full of sandwiches and soft drinks beside you while you drive, a decent sound system for some tunes, and room to stretch out in the back seat (or recline the front seat) when you need to take a break. Comfort may mean room for all your buddies on that road trip during spring break or to the lake. Or, comfort may mean having entertainment (DVDs or video games) for the kids, room for the dog and a bunch of luggage, and a leather-wrapped steering wheel for you to keep your hands around lest they go around someone's neck.

Whatever your automotive upholstery needs, this book will help you meet those needs, whether you design, sew, and install the interior yourself or have a professional do it. Even if you hire a professional, knowing what is involved in achieving what you want will make the entire process more enjoyable.

# CHAPTER 1
# PLANNING THE INTERIOR SPACE

Although it is often overlooked, the interior space of your automobile is very important, whether you are a restorer or a customizer. It's natural to focus on a car's overall appearance—the paint color, the wheel and tire combination, and the engine (how clean it is, or how much of it protrudes through the hood). Outward appearance is important to most enthusiasts, whether they are sports car buffs, muscle car collectors, antique aficionados, or hot rodders. Yet going down the road, other people experience your vehicle's appearance more than you do. If it's a vehicle you use, the interior space should be equally or more important to you. Whether you are on a cross-country excursion or just cruisin' Main, you want to feel comfortable behind the wheel, or while riding shotgun. You probably want everyone in the vehicle to feel safe and secure too, especially if this is family transportation.

Not only should you be comfortable in the seat, you should (when driving) be able to operate controls comfortably and easily. The driver obviously should be able to adjust the seat to reach the throttle, brake, and, if equipped, the clutch pedal; fit beneath the steering wheel; and see over the dash. Passengers should be able to put their window up or down (manually or power assisted), direct heating and cooling ducts, and reach the door handle without being a contortionist.

The ability to change positions, if even just slightly, while on a long drive keeps you and your passengers happy. Even if you don't plan on sleeping in your vehicle, we all face times when it's great to recline the seat and catch a few winks during a break from driving or while a passenger.

On all but the first horseless carriages, seats have been adjustable in a forward and backward direction. Modern seats, particularly the driver's, can often be adjusted up and down as well to help motorists remain relaxed and in control. Other features such as tilt wheel, telescoping steering column, and adjustable pedals

The interior of this 1932 Ford roadster is simple without many frills. Everything serves its intended purpose without much extra nonsense. A slim-and-trim steering column takes up minimal floor space and legroom—especially important on an early hot rod with a manual transmission, floor shifter, and clutch pedal. Analog gauges in the dash are located where the driver easily can monitor them. A parking brake lever is located along the floor just in front of the passenger seat, while a deck lid release is mounted just in front of the driver seat.

This 2005 Chevrolet Equinox has many of the modern conveniences that we take for granted in a contemporary automobile. Most noticeable are the seats with lumbar support and headrests that are adjustable in the vertical direction. Seatbelts are incorporated into the seat itself. The lever below the seatbelt allows the seatback to be adjusted between straight up and near reclining. The lever in front of it ratchets to raise or lower the seat cushion. Also in view are a floor console, armrest, and tilt steering wheel.

enable a given vehicle to accommodate drivers of most any body shape or size.

Major automakers employ ergonomic designers to determine how best to make the interior features fit our bodies and lifestyles. They employ engineers to determine ways to keep road and engine noise out, while keeping climate-controlled air and the latest stereo sound in. Not that you should hire a staff of engineers to design the interior of your latest automotive project, but put some thought and planning into how to make it as comfortable as possible. This advanced thought will pay off in the long run if you plan to spend much time behind the wheel. Even if you are building a truly custom, one-off vehicle, make use of contemporary automotive engineering technological advances, rather than reinvent the wheel.

## DETERMINING THE SCOPE OF THE PROJECT

The type of vehicle you are working on and its intended purpose have a major impact on what needs to be done in regard to upholstery. Restoring an antique vehicle with minimal upholstery to its original condition is much simpler than outfitting a state-of-the-art hot rod with extensive seating, carpet, and all the conveniences of home.

Are you simply repairing or covering a cigarette burn or small tear in the original upholstery? Perhaps your desire is to cover the existing seats, but you want more than a slip-on seat cover. Maybe you need to rebuild the seat or simply replace the foam padding, or would you be better off replacing the seat? What if this vehicle is a complete,

This Model T Speedster would most likely be fun to drive . . . for awhile. The seats don't appear to be adjustable, have minimal padding, and force your legs to stick straight out.

*This interior is inviting and includes several design elements. The seats and door panels are covered in leather or a high-grade vinyl and appear to have ample padding. I would suspect that the center armrest includes some hidden storage. The armrest in the door has sufficient room to support your arm, can be used as a door pull, and, if you look closely, you can see that it houses a stereo speaker.*

frame-off rebuild and you are starting from scratch on the interior? Whether you do the work yourself or hire a professional, you will need to determine just what needs to be done in order to obtain the desired results. Careful planning at the start of the project keeps track of everything you have, everything you need, and helps you budget your time and money.

## Restoration

For the purposes of this book, the term "restoration" refers to the process of bringing a vehicle back to like-new condition by repairing, reconditioning, or replacing components to recreate their original style, pattern, and appearance. Whether the vehicle is a Ford Model A, a Mercedes-Benz, or a Ferrari, a thorough restoration means to repair or replace the upholstery (and all other components, as well) to match what was originally on the vehicle when it left the factory. Anything less than the correct pattern, colors, and materials counts against the vehicle in the eyes of a car show judge or potential buyer if the vehicle in question has been "restored." (Many vehicles have been rebuilt to a condition much better than "new," yet they cannot truly be considered "restored." This is a moot point to some, but a strong bone of contention to others.)

Most vehicles that are completely, authentically restored are in museums or private collections. In either case, the

*The interior of this Mustang has been restored to original, at least to the casual observer. The seats and door panels are covered with the original material in the original design. Early Mustang seats were never thought to be extremely comfortable. They have minimal padding and the seat back angle is not adjustable.*

vehicles are seldom if ever driven; therefore, the wear and tear of daily use usually does not enter into the equation.

Obviously, some enthusiasts are more concerned about perfect restoration than others. Many automotive hobbyists prefer not to go to the expense or level of detail required for a completely authentic restoration if they actually drive the vehicle. (Do you want to retain the original tires if they're unsafe? Or the original seat springs and padding if they don't support your legs and back?) These enthusiasts seek to improve upon what they feel is a good thing. They retain many of the items that give their particular vehicle its character such as specific options or trim levels. Yet they do not forego upgrades that may enhance the driving experience. Enough enthusiasts support this path to give many modified vehicles a higher selling price than their original or restored counterparts. The important thing is to have fun with the process and the outcome, regardless of the level of restoration you choose. Just be willing to accept the fact that someone, somewhere, may be quick to point out that an otherwise trivial detail on your vehicle may not be authentic if you claim that it is original or restored.

Restoring upholstery on some vehicles will involve only the seat and nothing else. Older vehicles had very little in the way of upholstery when compared to the luxurious vehicles of today. Even today's economy cars are much more sophisticated than most older vehicles. The newer a vehicle, the more upholstery-related items there will be to tend to while restoring the vehicle. Seats, carpet, door panels, headliner, convertible top, dash panel covering, weather stripping, door seals, and insulation all will be the responsibility of the person in charge of the upholstery restoration.

## Modification

Maybe restoration is not your goal. If you update, modernize, rebuild, hot rod, or just fix up an older vehicle, you can use whatever materials, styles, colors, or patterns you wish in order to achieve the vehicle of your dreams. As long as the interior and upholstery meet your needs, a modified vehicle is pretty much wide open to whatever you choose to do.

If installing a pair of bucket seats purchased at a swap meet makes that bench-seat-equipped, hand-me-down grocery getter a race car in your eyes, good for you. If some new foam and a set of slip-on seat covers from Pep Boys is all that your budget allows, that is okay too. That's not to say that you can't take your vehicle to an upholsterer for a completely new interior just because you want to. If you replace the carpet, adding new insulation to deaden road noise and minimize engine heat, it will be money well spent. A majority of our time with our cars is spent inside them, so the interior should be as nice as we want.

## New construction

If you are building (or more accurately, rebuilding) a vehicle from the ground up, your interior possibilities and choices are virtually endless when it comes to materials, colors, and patterns. You can create all sorts of luxury and convenience when you design a completely new interior. Seats can be

*Although this early Ford Thunderbird goes against the advice to use neutral colors in the interior, it does go well with the rest of the car. With this T-Bird being a collector car instead of a daily driver, chances are that the paint scheme won't be changed and the interior should look nice for a long time.*

*In addition to making a vehicle more plush than original, you can also go to the other extreme. The fabricated bomber-style seats in this roadster certainly become a focal point of this hot rod's interior. Although these aluminum seats may appear uncomfortable, they are quite the opposite. There is ample padding in the seat while the backs provide plenty of support, along with ventilation holes to keep you from sticking to the back.*

made as plush as your tastes and budget will allow. You can incorporate modern conveniences such as storage compartments, stereo, video and communication systems, and cup holders that were never included when a particular vehicle was originally built. DVD entertainment systems and an extensive assortment of accessories that plug into power outlets (formerly known as cigarette lighters) are now available from the automotive aftermarket, allowing you to build the ultimate auto interior. Some folks have even made custom luggage to fit the trunk of a particular hot rod.

The most important advice I can give to someone designing an interior is this: remember to make the vehicle functional. Functionality is not as common a problem with restorations or updates to production vehicles as it is on many street rods or custom vehicles that are intended more for show than for road use. A fuse panel can often be hidden behind an easily removed, upholstered panel that is more convenient than the under-dash placement that was common for so long. It is also easy to run ducting for rear seat air conditioning vents as long as you plan for it before the vehicle is upholstered. Just be sure that anything hidden behind upholstery is accessible for servicing. I have seen more than one vehicle that required removing the seat to replace a dead battery. On many hot rods, the master cylinder is located beneath the floor. This is all well and good, until you need to fill the master cylinder. If your

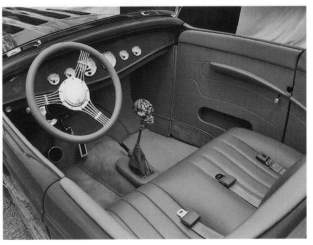

*On the other hand, this roadster features a plush interior. A bench seat with pleated leather, matching carpet, door panels with armrests that flow from the door panel to the side panel, and some storage areas make this a complete interior.*

vehicle fits into this scenario, consider using a remote fill to avoid having to pull up carpet or floor mats to access the master cylinder.

Whenever you build a custom vehicle or make significant changes to the stock configuration, do yourself a favor and sit in the vehicle prior to completing the interior. You may find that mounting the seat forward, backward, higher, or lower provides a better seating position. Maybe you need to move the armrest a bit higher or lower. Perhaps some extra foam in the seat cushion would make ingress and egress easier for an elderly person. Not that you would want to deviate far from the norm, but you should remember that major auto manufacturers try to fit everyone into their vehicles.

## DESIGNING THE INTERIOR SPACE

Whatever type of vehicle you work on, think of various areas of the vehicle as complete sections or subassemblies. These typically are the drivetrain, body, chassis, and so on. When you determine what modifications or upgrades to make to the engine, you naturally take the transmission into consideration as well. When prepping the body for paint, you direct your efforts toward a specific area (e.g., to repair collision or rust damage); however, you design the overall body paint scheme as one complete part.

Likewise, you will need to think of the interior as one complete unit as you decide which components to use. The seating, door panels, headliner, dash, and carpet all need to work together to provide a vehicle interior that you can be proud of. You can feel free to mix and match colors and textures when choosing material, although you should probably limit yourself to around three or four different materials. An example would be to use the same vinyl on the seats, headliner, and door panels. The door panel may also have a different color vinyl insert, and maybe a carpeted panel as well. This, of course, should match the carpet on the floor. To look the best, all these materials would be similar or complementary in color. Although there are exceptions, most colors used on interior surfaces are neutral in color or are a shade or two lighter than the exterior paint.

Just as you should not incorporate too many different colors or textures, you should limit the number of patterns as well. Having a traditional roll-and-pleated door panel would not look right when combined with a seat that is stitched in diamond pleats with buttons. In similar fashion, you wouldn't want to combine a crushed velour seat with door panels covered with vinyl. All rules are made to be broken, but it seems appropriate not to use more than two patterns in any one vehicle, one of which would simply be smooth (but padded) material.

Obviously, the number of components varies depending on the vehicle, but have you looked inside a contemporary automobile lately? There is much more than just a steering wheel, gauges, shifter, and seats. Air conditioning and stereo equipment add controls (temperature and fan speed,

*The door panel of this Chevrolet Beretta includes different materials that work well together. The lower half of the panel is covered with the same carpet as the floor, with a lighter color velour material on the back half of the top to balance the dark gray vinyl on the portion of the panel that would be more difficult to cover due to the door latch mechanism.*

as well as volume and other selection controls) and outlets (vents or speakers). It isn't necessary to make these items completely invisible, but you should try to make them look like they were designed to be part of the interior package rather than a complete afterthought. A simple way to improve the looks of an aftermarket air conditioning unit is to paint the louvers (vents) to match the rest of the interior components. This can be easily done with automotive paint designed to be applied to vinyl interior pieces. Other items such as door handles and window riser mechanisms, remote mirror adjusters, seatbelts, cup holders, and storage areas also deserve prior planning and a method of detailing if they are included.

### Seats

The primary concern for choosing a seat is that it is comfortable. If you are restoring a vehicle to its original condition, you may be stuck with a less-than-comfortable seating arrangement. If the seating is very uncomfortable, you may have to decide between an authentic "restoration" or a "fix-up." If you are intent on accurately restoring a vehicle, you can restore it with optional seating that was available, but not originally in your vehicle.

Let's assume that you are upgrading an existing seat, or perhaps even choosing a new seat for a complete vehicle rebuild. If the seat needs more padding, add it. The existing foam simply may be worn out so if the seat needs more padding, by all means have more foam installed before the new seat covers are made. If the driver of the vehicle is petite and has trouble reaching the pedals, rework the seat mounting mechanisms to allow the seat to sit closer to the floor. On the other hand, maybe the seat needs to sit higher so that the driver can better see over the hood.

For customized vehicles, ask owners of similar vehicles about their seating: Do they like it, and would they use the same seating again if they had it to do over? Ask to sit inside their vehicle to make your own judgment. I recently asked a hot rodder how he liked the high-dollar, highly acclaimed seating that was in his coupe. He was quick to say that it wasn't as comfortable as he felt it should be for the price. He noted that we are not all the same size and shape, so we will not all be comfortable in the same seat. Although it certainly wasn't intentional on my part, I walked away feeling bad because I had obviously brought up a sore subject. Don't be afraid to ask around before you make your buying decision—even a popular product may not be ideal for a given person.

This previous situation is a good reason for buying new seat frames and foam that are not upholstered and then having them covered locally (or at least by the person doing your upholstery work), rather than new seats that are ready to bolt into place. If the seats are not yet covered, you can sit in them to gain a better perspective of slight changes that would make your drive time more comfortable. You can then discuss these changes with your upholsterer who can probably add some foam here or there to make things more comfortable before the covers go on.

Many companies that make seat frames or do custom upholstery work display their wares at large automotive events and welcome potential customers to test out their seats. I must admit that I have been thankful for this while at some large events. Keep in mind, though, that if you are dead on your feet from walking around on pavement all day looking at cars, most anywhere you can sit for a moment and take a load off will seem comfy. The real test will be how this new seat feels while in the confines of your car, as you hold onto your steering wheel. If your better half enters the garage to find you simply sitting behind the wheel and accuses you of wasting time, you can reply that you are planning.

Keep in mind that changes in one area will have effects elsewhere. Adding foam to the bottom cushion reduces headroom. Adding foam to the back cushion moves you that much closer to the steering wheel and pedals. If you've removed the top during work, fit it in its proper location when you make seating decisions. You may be able to make an offsetting change to get what you want—for example, fitting seat frames that adjust up and down, or remounting the seat frame further back. To borrow a phrase from the carpenters, "measure twice, cut once."

Will there be one driver or several for this vehicle? Is this your personal "driving is a form of relaxation" vehicle, or is this the one vehicle that all your teenage kids are to share as they go through high school and college? If you are building the vehicle for just one person (as a race car might be), the seating can be and often is customized specifically for that person. If necessary, extra foam can be used on one side or the other to help accommodate someone who has had physical ailments or surgery that may require extra support. If it is just for you, you can make it to your exact specifications.

If the entire family is driving the car, you will be better off in the long run minimizing the luxuries and maximizing the function. Read that as bench seats with lots of adjustability and durable material. The seat will need to have a larger adjustment range. Quite simply, our legs and arms are not all the same length, and some of us sit higher in the seat than others. All the vehicle's drivers must be able to reach the pedals, steering wheel, and other controls; see over the dash; and use the rearview mirror. For these three reasons, the ideal seat is adjustable front to back, up and down, and in tilt angle. As an example, I am six foot one, but have short legs and a long torso. When the seat is adjusted adequately to reach the pedals, I am sometimes too close to the steering wheel or, more often, don't have comfortable headroom. If I can lower the seat or tilt it backward, I can usually still reach the pedals and steering wheel while gaining some headroom.

When you think about it, there are many things to consider when designing the interior space of your automobile, and all those items are multiplied by the number of possible drivers. Even the slight differences between someone who is five foot six and someone who is six foot two can make a difference in optimal seating position. You must also consider rear seat legroom if your vehicle has back seats. The amount of legroom that suits children may not be enough for adult passengers. This fact may affect your decision of where to place the front seats, or what type of seating track and adjustments to use.

## Consoles

Years ago, the glove compartment was about the only storage space in a vehicle besides the trunk. Does anyone actually keep gloves in the glove box anymore? As the motoring public began spending more time in their vehicles for fun and business, all sorts of storage compartments were added. Everything from seat covers with built-in map pockets and plastic consoles with rubber feet to help prevent sliding, to drywall mud buckets and Tupperware containers have been used to organize or minimize the clutter in the interiors of our vehicles—not to mention cup holders. What did we ever do without them?

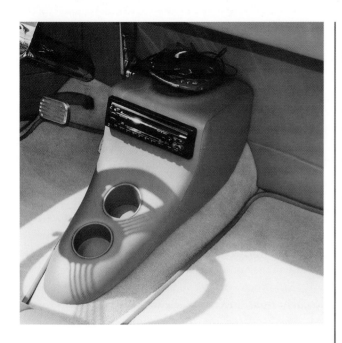

*This console serves as an extension to the main dash to house air conditioning controls, an A/C vent, a couple of switches, and an interior courtesy light on either side. Above the oval air conditioning control panel are high beam and turn signal indicator lights. Note how padded vinyl covers the console to match the seats and dash.*

*This console is not overly complicated, yet is a tasteful addition to this roadster. It houses a stereo and provides a couple of cup holders. What more could you need while cruising in a hot rod roadster?*

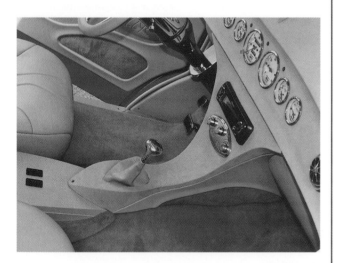

*Covered with carpet and vinyl, this console mirrors the pattern of the door panels. On many street rods, the dash simply doesn't have enough room for gauges and modern-day conveniences such as air conditioning and stereo, and in this case a floor shifter.*

a variety of other options. A look inside a contemporary minivan or sport utility vehicle shows items such as CD (or now even DVD) players and storage for their respective media, coin holders, plug-in power supplies for toys and games, cup holders, map lights, and garage door openers. If you are modifying a vehicle anyway, there is no reason why you cannot incorporate some of these items in your "new" interior. You can even purchase aftermarket satellite stereo systems, so if you make many cross-country trips or drive in areas where local radio leaves something to be desired, a new console may be the perfect addition to your vehicle.

Since more vehicles are being OEM-equipped with floor and overhead consoles, a trip to a salvage yard may provide just the perfect console for your older vehicle. If you are exchanging a bench seat for a pair of bucket seats, the source of the buckets may have just the console you need and be a direct bolt-in at that. Even if you are using aftermarket seats, a salvage yard may yield a console that will meet your needs with little to no additional work. This may be easier than fabricating something from scratch. Even if you don't find something usable, seeing original equipment items may give you ideas for fabricating your own console.

Depending on how creative you are and how well stocked your favorite salvage yard is, you may be able to incorporate a portion of an OEM console into your own

The true inventor of the automobile's overhead or floor console may be forgotten, but he or she has made life on the road more convenient. Besides housing a stereo in an overhead console and a shifter in a floor console, these "extra" compartments can also be used to house or conceal

The interior of this 1948 Chevrolet pickup looks more like a contemporary vehicle's than its original utilitarian equipment. It's unknown if the console is from the same vehicle as the seats, but the two components work well together. The height of the console eliminates the possibility of third-person seating, yet provides a center armrest. When planning your interior, decide what will best suit your needs.

This same Chevrolet pickup shows a basically stock dash configuration, although it has some custom features. A stereo has been installed in the portion of the dash that originally housed the stock radio speaker. New gauges are in the stock location, but in custom aluminum housings. An aftermarket air conditioning unit is mounted under the dash and has been painted to match the dash.

Lots of non-stock items are housed in this floor console. A couple of air conditioning vents, a pair of gauges, power window switches, and an air conditioning control panel are all included. The console also mounts a pair of stereo speakers and cup holders.

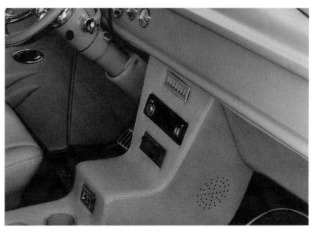

Although the dash appears to have plenty of available space, a console is used to mount the stereo and air conditioning controls. It also mounts an A/C vent and stereo speaker on each side. Although it wouldn't be as necessary on a street rod, heat vents aimed toward the floor can be a nice touch for any vehicle that may be driven in cooler weather.

overall design. An example of this might be to graft the top portion of a console that has two cup holders and a lockable storage unit onto your own custom base.

Bear in mind that incorporating some of these conveniences will require more work than others. Storage compartments, map pockets, and coin holders are simple to construct. Other conveniences such as stereos, video games, lighting equipment, and power supplies require electrical wiring. This is not a big deal by any means; it's merely something you will need to plan for. You will need to have

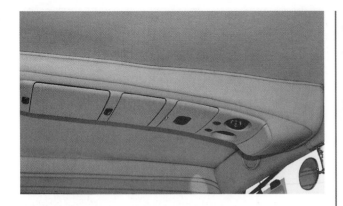

*This overhead console houses several different items—just what they are is unknown until the vehicle's owner opens each component. A guess would be that the console houses a DVD player for rear seat passengers and a garage door opener.*

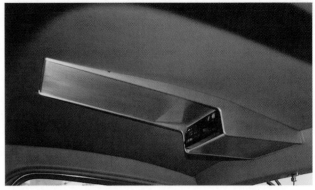

*An aluminum console in this coupe is plain and simple but is used only to house a stereo. The horizontal section near the center of the roof would be an ideal location for rocker switches for power windows, power door locks, or other electric accessories.*

*By lifting the center armrest in this Chevrolet Equinox, we find storage dedicated to CDs and a handy place for a box of tissues. Not something that macho guys need, but my wife loves all the conveniences of her new SUV.*

*At the back of the center armrest are cup holders for rear seat passengers and a power outlet for a multitude of time-occupying devices. Even though the driver may never use these conveniences, comfortable passengers make for a more enjoyable driving experience.*

all the wiring completed prior to upholstery work. To avoid a common problem, verify that you have provided a good ground for electrical components. It is much easier to locate and correct a wiring problem before the upholstery work is completed. Make sure your electrical wiring is properly routed, will not get pinched, and passes through rubber grommets rather than bare sheet metal so that it doesn't get stripped and short out over time.

## Dash

Unless you are doing a complete rebuild, you most likely won't change the dash very much, if any. This doesn't mean you have to live with a dash that's cracked, deformed, or

*If you ever need to jack up a vehicle anywhere other than your garage or driveway, you want the vehicle's jack stored in a place that is easy to get to. Simply pull out this small panel located just inside the rear hatch. Easy to get to, but out of sight, makes for a good design.*

*Simply pull the cover off to access the jack. This vehicle's good use of available storage areas makes it more user-friendly.*

faded. Depending on the vintage of the vehicle, you may choose to upholster or paint the dash. With later model vehicles, the most practical route likely will be replacing the factory-padded dash. Replacement dash pads are available for most popular vehicles.

Even if you do not make any changes to the dash, a thorough cleaning can make a big difference. The dash panel(s) is usually held in place with small screws, so disassembly is relatively easy. Wiping away the fine dust that works its way into what seems like a sealed compartment can improve the looks of your dash panel. Often, the clear plastic that covers the instrument cluster becomes cloudy or even cracked. Although you may have to do some research to find a replacement for your particular vehicle,

*Most of the components that would be necessary to restore the dash and interior of this 1960s muscle car are available from an ever-growing aftermarket.*

*The dash in this convertible is purely custom, as is much of the car. Gauge placement stretches much of the way across the dash, which could make for some difficulty in reading those last couple of gauges from the driver's position.*

these panels are readily available and are just the finishing touch for a new interior.

On the other hand, if you are building your version of the perfect automobile, the dash is a great place to show your creativity and express your individuality. Whether you are transplanting an entirely different dash or modifying what is already there, remember that you will be looking at this new dash during your entire time behind the wheel, so plan accordingly. Place gauges where you can easily read them, controls where you can reach them, and dashboard illumination where it can light what it is supposed to without blinding you. Turn signal and high-beam indicators do not have to be large to be seen. When placed appropriately, indicator lights that are but a sixteenth of an inch in diameter will quickly and efficiently serve their purpose without being obtrusive. An indicator light that is too large can become more of a distraction than a benefit if its brightness overpowers other dash illumination.

## Additional considerations

Beyond their functionality, items such as the steering wheel and gauges serve as fashion accessories to the overall concept of your upholstery. The steering wheel and gauges set the mood for the interior and are the first thing our eye sees when we enter or look inside. Is your vehicle race car-inspired, more of a restored classic, stock as a rock, or somewhere in between? You should note that the rest of your vehicle should reflect the interior and vice versa. If you are resurrecting an early-1970s Barracuda to its original muscle car appearance, you wouldn't want to use an early

*This photo shows a couple of items that may not seem like a big deal but are modern conveniences that are missed if we don't have them. A heat vent in the floor area (near the middle of the photo) helps to keep your toes (therefore the rest of your body) warm on those frosty mornings. Second is a small storage area in the dash ideal for sunglasses.*

Ford banjo wheel or an aftermarket billet aluminum wheel. You wouldn't want to use a polished aluminum aftermarket steering column. In similar fashion, you wouldn't want to use race car-inspired gauges in the family's grocery-getter sedan, or vintage-looking gauges in your import tuner car.

Gauge placement certainly can be changed; however, from a practical standpoint, the gauges should be where they are readily visible from the driver seat. This is not so

*The dash in this 1939 Ford coupe has a definite art-deco look. A piece of stainless trim flanks the gauges and provides some extra dazzle to the dash. A chrome steering column highlights the otherwise painted dash.*

*The gauge placement in the author's Chevrolet Silverado is not flashy, but there is nothing wrong with it. All gauges are easily seen from the driver's position. Being analog, they are not subject to lighting conditions that sometimes hinder the ability to read digital gauges.*

much of a concern when reupholstering the daily driver, but can make a bold statement when constructing a custom car. In many of the import tuner cars seen on the street today, warning lights are replaced with gauges mounted on the windshield/door pillar. Since these are more in line with the driver's line of sight, this is probably an improvement over accessory under-dash panels common in the past.

It seems strange that many high-performance muscle cars from the 1960s were still equipped with warning lights

*These aftermarket gauges are used in addition to the OEM gauges in a four-wheel-drive truck to monitor a warmed-up diesel engine. Modified engines may require more gauges to monitor their operation properly than the engine in your daily driver. In this case, the extra gauges are mounted on the windshield pillar, making them easy for the driver to read.*

rather than gauges. Factory gauges were usually an option that young shoppers deemed too expensive. Ultimately, however, they would determine that gauges were indeed a good idea on a high-performance vehicle, and would add an aftermarket gauge cluster. Most guys mounted these below the dash in a less-than-practical location. If you cannot see the gauge, it isn't very effective. (If you're doing a restoration and would like gauges offered for your car, but not on it, explore a wrecking yard with the appropriate dash before redoing the interior.)

A note about gauges: Digital gauges are becoming more common in vehicles. They are available in a variety of colors and work well in closed cars such as sedans, coupes, and SUVs. Depending on the color chosen, however, digital gauges can sometimes be difficult to read in open vehicles. This is not an attempt to discourage you from using digital gauges, but consider the point while you are designing that perfect interior. Again, ask other vehicle owners about their experiences and what they would suggest if they were going to do their car over. Some colors are easier to see than others, so if you feel that you must have digital gauges, changing colors may be appropriate.

### CHOOSING YOUR LOOK

Now that you realize some of the not-so-obvious things that you need to consider when planning your interior, you can begin thinking about the more obvious aspects of your impending upholstery job. These items are the material, color, style, pattern, and layout. Even if sewn together by the greatest of upholsterers, poor-quality materials will not withstand constant wear. Wild colors will go out of style eventually and less-than-pleasing patterns will quickly grow old. For the cost of having a high-quality upholstery job, it pays to give some thought to all the variables before plunking down your money. Even if you are doing the work yourself, the cost of materials and your time warrant proper planning.

### Choosing material

As mentioned previously, perfect restorations require use of the original material, regardless of its durability or difficulty in finding and working with it. It may be leather, Mohair, vinyl, or any of a number of other materials. You will need to research the particular vehicle to find out the original materials, colors, and style or pattern. Of course, if you are doing a complete restoration, you probably already realize that, as you have no doubt researched all the other aspects of the vehicle already.

On any vehicle that you are modifying, you can use whatever material suits your taste and falls within your budget. This opens up a wide variety of choices that fall

*Although it is not as popular as it once was, tweed makes for nice upholstery material, as shown in this 1934 Ford coupe. The bench seat, door panels, and headliner are all covered with tweed. Tweed is very easy to work with, available in a wide variety of colors, and relatively inexpensive. A downside is that tweed is not as durable as leather or heavier vinyl. These characteristics make it a good choice for a special-interest vehicle that sees only limited use.*

within a much wider range of prices. Most materials come in different grades, so even if you can't afford (or justify) top-quality leather, you can probably find something similar that is a little less expensive. Many people can't tell leather from better grades of vinyl anyway, so if you can't tell the difference, why pay the difference?

In the late 1980s and early 1990s, tweed material was very popular among the hot rod crowd, whether it was in late-model cars, street rods, or trucks. This material is easy to work with, can be glued to a variety of panel materials, and comes in a wide range of colors. It was common to have an upholsterer stitch the seat covers and the owner spray glue on a door panel and fit the tweed material to it.

Because tweed was so user-friendly, many folks added "upholsterer" to their resumes. Once you mastered the standard door panel, it was easy enough to make fancier, sculpted panels by gluing layers of foam onto the panel, shaping the raised portion of foam, and covering it all with tweed material. This material allowed many enthusiasts to do their own upholstery and also gave upholsterers more freedom with their design process. Even though the current material of choice is more along the lines of leather, the sculpted interiors that are found on late-model vehicles are largely due to the advances made in automotive interiors when tweed was the rage. Even though it may not be as popular as it once was, tweed is easy to work with and is certainly inexpensive enough for the beginner upholsterer. A drawback of tweed is that in all but the very lightest of colors, it can feel very hot—not like the heat of a black vinyl seat that has been sitting in the sun, but more of a suffocating heat, especially in a coupe or sedan.

At the turn of the 21st century, leather and leather looka-likes became popular. Natural leather is very durable and certainly gives the impression of high quality and style. It's expensive, however, and is therefore not the ideal material to learn on. If you want leather's look but not its price, don't despair, as there are alternatives. Man-made leather-like materials such as Naugahyde and Ultraleather are sometimes more suitable for automotive interiors and available at a fraction of the cost. This doesn't mean they are cheap, but they are usually less expensive than real cowhide. These man-made materials are also good in larger vehicles, as sometimes a cow just isn't big enough to cover the entire area to be upholstered.

On the lesser end of the price scale is vinyl, making it the most common material for automotive interiors. When ordering, make sure you specify automotive grade vinyl as it is manufactured with UV tolerances that are necessary for automotive use. Automotive grade vinyl comes in three weights: service, standard, and expanded. For areas that will see little wear or abrasion, such as headliners or backs of seats, service grade is suitable. Areas such as door panels may require the use of the thicker standard weight vinyl. Seating surfaces and other areas subjected to constant wear should be covered with expanded vinyl, which is made more flexible and durable by having a cloth backing. Of course, to minimize inventory, some upholsterers use expanded vinyl for all their jobs. Using the same grade of vinyl throughout the vehicle helps eliminate slight differences in color or texture that may otherwise occur. The one drawback is that material durable enough for seating will require extra support when used for headliners.

When choosing material for your automotive upholstery

*This is one of those interiors that looks better in photos than in reality. Ill-fitting, cheap seat covers have been installed over some thoroughly trashed seats. The carpets have several stains and the vinyl dash pad has some small cracks. Who knows what may be lurking under the seats or under the carpet?*

project, look for something that would be more suitable for the family room in your house, rather than a formal dining room. The interior of your vehicle is likely to be subjected to most everything that your family room is and then some. The formal dining room may look exquisite, but quite honestly won't last without constant maintenance. Your vehicle's interior may be subjected to all of the following at one time or another: French fries, cigarettes, lipstick, soft drinks, pets, candy bars, rain, mud, dust, dirt, road salt, and bubblegum. Obviously, a special-interest vehicle may not be subjected to all these items, but you can sure bet that a daily driven family sedan will be.

In addition to the material used to cover the seats, door panels, and headliner, you will need carpet on the floor. Just like all other materials, carpet comes in a variety of grades and prices. How the material wears and how much the vehicle is used should be among the deciding factors when choosing carpet. In lieu of carpet, some utilitarian vehicles (construction vehicles and other off-road vehicles) are better served by removable rubber floor mats.

## Choosing colors

Now that you have all your interior's gadgets and conveniences planned out and you have decided what type of material fits your budget, what color should you pick? Conventional wisdom says to choose a color that is complementary or contrasting to the exterior color. If that still doesn't answer

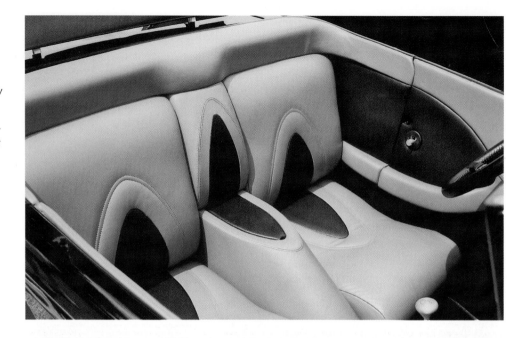

*Tan and dark gray vinyl covers the interior of this street rod convertible. Both colors are neutral and could be used with most any exterior color. Note how minimal pattern stitching provides a super smooth surface. The pattern is carried throughout the seats and the door panels.*

*This brightly colored interior looks great, is well done, utilizes top craftsmanship, and goes nicely with the current exterior color. However, if the current owner or a potential buyer would like a different exterior color, the interior would need to be reupholstered to coordinate with all but a handful of colors.*

your question, it would be wise to choose a neutral or earth-toned color. Choose a color that will suit whatever exterior color you may choose for this vehicle during the time you plan to own it. Grays and browns come in a wide variety of shades, making them popular interior colors.

When choosing a color for the interior, be careful about matching colors. Even though the exterior is a different material (steel/fiberglass) than the interior (mostly cloth/vinyl) and will therefore cause some difference in appearance, certain differences in colors will cause an unpleasant clash. Automakers put a lot of effort into coloring the various interior surfaces—plastic, vinyl, metal, carpet—so they match and appear consistent across various lighting conditions. It's a difficult goal to achieve for all of a manufacturer's color

options. For example, sometimes a car will combine a maroon or wine-colored interior with a red exterior. I have seen several such vehicles where the overall effect was more of a clash than a complement. Another tricky combination is to match certain shades of blue with blue/green teal. One way to avoid this is to have a small piece of sheet metal painted the same color as your car. This painted piece (more handy than a fender or deck lid) can then be taken to the upholstery shop for comparisons with material swatches. To be on the safe side, compare the two materials in sunlight and in shade.

A common design approach is to use two colors in the interior of a vehicle that has a single exterior color, and a single color in the interior of a two-toned vehicle. Whether these combinations are attractive will depend on the colors involved and the styling of the particular vehicle. Old Corvettes and Austin Healeys often came from the factory with two-tone paint, but Honda Civics and VW GTIs did not. There are no set rules when it comes to choosing colors, as whatever rules may have applied at one point have been broken already—sometimes with effective results, and sometimes not. You'll have to live with your decision, so choose carefully.

One way to give customers (or yourself) a better idea of what colors look good together is to use a paint color "wheel" in conjunction with upholstery samples. These color wheels are available at most home paint stores and have at least slightly larger color swatches than most automotive paint color charts. Ideally, the otherwise finished vehicle with the exterior and interior colors already painted would be available when choosing upholstery colors, but realistically, this isn't always the case.

A complete interior is a substantial investment and as such should last for quite some time. Whether by choice (you never did really like the color of that car anyway) or by accident (somebody wrecked your car so now it needs to be repainted), you may choose to change the exterior color of your car. If you just had the interior done in lime green or purple, about the only choice you have for the exterior

is . . . lime green or purple. If that new interior is done in a tasteful gray, tan, or a cross between the two, your choices for a repaint color are nowhere near as limited. This is especially something to consider if you plan to fix up the car and then sell it. Even if the for sale sign goes in the window before the lime green paint is dry and the matching interior hasn't been sat upon yet, the potential buyer may not plan to keep the lime green paint forever.

## Choosing a style, pattern, and layout

The overall style of the vehicle itself will influence the style, pattern, and layout of your new upholstery. If you are building a retro-styled, no frills hot rod, you most likely wouldn't stitch the interior with tweed over power bucket seats and sculpted door panels. Likewise, if you are resurrecting a Porsche or Ferrari sports car, you wouldn't want to upholster it with a Tijuana tuck-and-roll trim job that would be more at home in a 1950s-era lead sled.

Even if you aren't a car show type person and are just making some repairs to your daily driver, it may do you good to check out a local car show or cruise night to see what other folks are doing with their automotive interiors to make them more comfortable.

These Cobra bucket seats are seen being upholstered elsewhere in this book. Unlike most seats that are comprised of a seat frame covered with foam and material, these start as a one-piece fiberglass shell. The seat cushion is a separate piece of foam that is covered and merely sits in place, while foam is glued to the seat back and sides, and then is covered with material.

Being race car-inspired, the interior of this Cobra is rather Spartan. No A/C, stereo, or cup holders to contend with. In some vehicles, driving is the reason for driving.

*Lots of knobs, switches, and gauges are located in a small area in this early Corvette. All operating controls are well within reach or plain sight of the driver, while the passenger has adequate legroom and a great view of the road.*

*The seat of this 1932 Ford roadster features a fold-down center armrest, square pleated seat, and a smooth vinyl roll around the upper edge of the body. Two different materials, velour and vinyl, combine for a tasteful interior.*

*The black-and-white vinyl interior in this 1932 Ford Tudor sedan has a nostalgic look. Relatively thin and straight back bucket seats appear to be from an early Mustang, but may be from another source. Notice how the contrasting black piping carries through on the door panels as well as the seats.*

*An aftermarket split-back bench seat found in a hot rod coupe. In addition to their nice pattern and leather upholstery, the seats are finished with a piece of polished trim to conceal the seat slider mechanisms. This trim may have been created especially for these seats; however, it is likely that they are OEM pieces that have been adapted to the seats.*

Adjustable headrests and lateral support are two of the extra features of these particular seats. These are most likely OEM seats that have been recovered for this vehicle. Note the three-point seatbelts in this street rod.

Plain, simple, and tasteful describe this red vinyl bench seat. Its traditional styling matches that of the black 1932 Ford roadster perfectly. Simple tuck and roll is relatively easy to do and looks great. Note how the pleats cover only approximately half of the seat cushion and seat back, while the front edge of the seat and top of the back are smooth.

The longer pleats on this bench seat give the interior a much different look than the shorter pleats on the preceding photo, even though the vehicles are basically the same. These pleats are also narrower, which makes them look even longer.

Light gray and white vinyl combine to make a great-looking interior in this Model A Tudor. The door panels are pleated to match the seats in a simple, timeless pattern.

Perhaps not suitable for a family sedan that gets lots of use, light buckskin leather bucket seats sure look nice on this street rod. Note that the pleats fan out from the middle, rather than being parallel.

Balance in this interior is achieved by combining a satin black–painted dash and floor console and lighter gray/white upholstery. The satin finish of the paint gives an entirely different look than if it were glossy black. Notice how the oval shape of the seat bolsters is repeated on the pad on the center armrest and the door panel armrests.

# CHAPTER 2
# WHO WILL DO THE WORK?

Okay, you have decided what your ride needs to commute to work, cruise the boulevard, or make the show circuit. Now you need to decide who will sew the materials together and make that dream come true. It could be that you will do it yourself. Also, your local telephone directory may lead you to companies in your area that do this kind of work; however, you may have to do some looking. Since many upholsterers either do this work as a hobby or are busy enough that they don't need to advertise, you may not find many advertisements in the local newspaper or local directory. If you know anyone who belongs to a local car club, he or she may be able to steer you toward a good upholsterer in your area. If all of the above resources fail, check out a local car show and ask car owners for references. For your daily driver, you should be able to find someone in your area who does suitable trim work. If you are building a one-off custom or street rod, it is not uncommon to hire upholsterers from several states away. For the latter case, expect to pay the extra bucks that a nationwide reputation commands.

## A PROFESSIONAL

Other than the upfront expense, it is usually good advice to hire a professional any time you need to have a service done. The expense of hiring a professional may seem steep at the time, but it will often be less than the total expense of not hiring a professional. Underestimating the time required to complete the job or miscalculating the costs are the typical pitfalls of hiring someone who is less than professional at their job. This is not to say that the person you hire to do your upholstery work has to have a storefront and do this work full time. Many good, longtime upholsterers do their work as a hobby. Many of them work at other professions full time because they don't want to rely on their own business while raising a family and paying a mortgage. Quite often, doing upholstery work on the side provides them with spending money for their own car hobby/habit. If they have become good at it and build a good reputation, automotive upholstery can serve as a good part-time/retirement income.

Unless someone in your family or circle of friends has already been doing upholstery work, you probably will not

If you are contemplating your first upholstery job, start on something other than an interior like this. Not that you couldn't do it, but this interior involves several components that may overwhelm a beginner. The bucket seats have a pattern that involves sewing together several pieces just to make the seat covers in addition to the headrests. There is also a center console/armrest to deal with. Door panels include a pleated insert, an armrest, and a colored insert. And we haven't even seen the headliner or carpet.

have all the necessary equipment to do automotive upholstery work yourself. Unless you plan on getting into this business yourself, you will most likely need to find a professional upholsterer to do your trim work.

As you obtain estimates from potential trimmers, they should provide satisfactory answers to more questions than just "how much?" You will need to find out how soon they can get started. You will also need to know that you can get your share of the work done prior to the time that they are ready to begin. This is not so much of a problem if you are just having a new headliner or seat covers installed. However, if this is a total rebuild, you will need to have a lot of work completed prior to dropping the vehicle off at the upholstery shop.

Can the potential upholsterer show you samples of their work? Don't be afraid to ask for a list of people to contact who have had work done by this particular trimmer. Contact those people to arrange a time to see their vehicles. Find out how long ago the work was done. Does the interior still look nice? How is it holding up? Keep in mind that the lifestyle of the person using the vehicle will have a great impact on how the inside of the vehicle appears after some time. Take this into consideration when looking at someone else's vehicle. Were they pleased with the quality and the price? Are the seams straight? Do pleats line up correctly from the seat cushion to the seat back? Were there any problems getting the work done within the agreed timeframe?

## When can they get started?

Most high-quality trimmers have a waiting list of work lined up ranging from a couple of weeks to close to a year or more in length. So don't wait until you are ready to have someone reupholster your entire vehicle to begin looking for someone to do the work. If you are indeed ready to have the upholstery work done on your vehicle, you like their work, and the price is suitable, you should probably go ahead and make the commitment so you can get on the waiting list. You may just have to wait awhile to get your upholstery work completed. If you think your vehicle is ready to upholster, but you are on a waiting list, ask the proposed upholsterer if there is anything you could do while you wait that would benefit you and the upholsterer. If you have another vehicle available, perhaps you can remove the seats to be upholstered, rather than paying the trimmer to do this basic task. Perhaps you could remove the carpet and check for rust in the floors, instead of the upholsterer finding the rust, which then prolongs the project. Show the upholsterer that you are willing to work with him or her and you may be able to save yourself a few bucks.

## Prior to dropping your vehicle at the upholsterer's shop

What do you need to have done prior to taking your vehicle to the upholsterer? The following items need to be completed, prior to leaving your vehicle with the upholsterer, whether it is a restoration, a daily driver, or a complete rebuild.

All wiring needs to be completed and thoroughly checked to verify that everything actually works as intended. Verify that wiring is routed behind structural supports, rather than between the support and the upholstered panel. If the wiring is located between the support and the upholstered panel, it will most likely leave an unsightly bulge if not corrected. So, route the wiring correctly (whether you do it yourself or someone else does it). Leave some slack in all the wiring—but not so much that it looks sloppy—so that upholstered panels can be accurately positioned. If you're not sure on this point, ask the upholsterer about it. There may be a car in the shop that can serve as an example of how proper wiring should look. During the job, upholsterers can certainly add a cable tie here and there if needed, but they don't want to wire the vehicle.

Avoid bundled wires running along the floorboard as you don't want passengers to think that a snake has been trapped below your carpet. If possible, run necessary wiring above the passenger compartment between the inside of the roof and the headliner. If there is no way around it, run the wiring along the floor in smaller bundles and route them along the door opening so that they can be covered by the door sill plate, instead of the carpet. On some vehicles where wiring runs across the floor out of necessity, we have seen the wires laid out flat on the floor (rather than in a round bundle), and then held in place with duct tape. The tape holds the wires flat against the floor and also serves to protect them somewhat.

Stereo components, tuner, amplifier, and speakers should all be located and mounted, if possible. The upholsterer may need to do the actual mounting of the speakers, but you should verify this well in advance. The same considerations used for wiring should apply to the stereo and related components as well.

Any consoles (overhead or floor mounted) and their related mounting should be secured in place. If the console is to be upholstered, make sure that its construction allows for this to be done. If it needs to be removed to be upholstered, can it be reinstalled easily? Do you need to rethink your mounting procedure? You should also verify with the upholsterer that their covering of any consoles will allow the console to be removed should it be necessary to access or service the equipment mounted in the console.

Seats that you plan to have upholstered should be bolted in place using the proper hardware. Although the

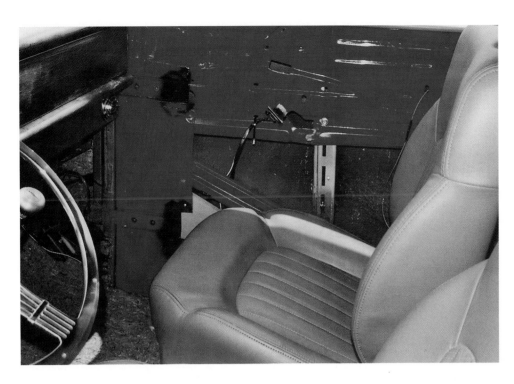

An interior in progress. The seats are covered, the dash is roughed in, and the wires are routed for the power windows. The power window switches will be mounted in the door panel that is yet to be finished.

upholsterer most likely will remove the seats before work begins, they should be delivered to the upholsterer in their intended location. You should also mount the seatbelts. Bolts for seatbelts usually thread into a nut welded to the underside of the floor, or into a tapped hole in a thick portion of the floor. If the seatbelts need to be removed or replaced, it is a good idea to somehow mark the bolt hole or threaded insert, so that its location can be easily found when reinstalling the seatbelts. New carpet will not have a hole in it, so it will be necessary to locate the hole from underneath by using an ice pick, awl, or small screwdriver.

Dashboard, garnish moldings, and the steering column are all items that may be painted, wood grained, chrome plated, or upholstered. Whatever final finish you choose for these parts should be completed before upholstery work begins. That way, you won't mess up the new upholstery job. Depending on the vehicle, the upholsterer may request that some of these items not be installed initially, but that should be discussed early on. An open line of communication between customer and craftsman is always important.

The upholsterer may insist on installing the sound dampening and insulation material if they are going to install the carpet. Check with them ahead of time to verify that they will install it if you don't. Don't assume that they will include it, as some trimmers prefer not to deal with it.

Window glass and the related sealants, moldings, and trim should be installed. If not actually installed, the interior door handles and window riser handles should be given to the upholsterer directly or located where they can be found easily.

Make sure you plan ahead and have the vehicle ready for the upholsterer when they are ready for you and your vehicle. If you realize that delays on your part are imminent, notify the upholsterer so that their schedule can be adjusted accordingly. They will probably be understanding if you let them know that you are running behind. Depending on what you are having done, they may even be able to go ahead and start on a portion of the work for your vehicle. However, if they have turned away work because they were planning on you being ready and then you don't show up at the last minute, you won't be gaining any popularity points.

## How soon can they complete the job?

Don't expect your new upholstery work to be completed overnight. If you have a specific time frame, make sure the upholsterer is aware of that from the beginning. Halfway into the project is not the time to bring up deadlines. If they tell you that they cannot finish the work in time for your deadline, find someone else to do the work or revise your time frame. Remember, lack of planning on your part does not constitute an emergency on their part. Communication is important; you should have lots of it when you determine the concept, design, and layout of your upholstery project, but you should remember to not pester the person doing the work. All the time spent listening to you could be better spent actually getting the work done.

## How much will it cost?

Anytime that you are shopping for professional services, it is wise to get a few, if not several, estimates. A common rule of thumb on any kind of estimate is to disregard the highest and lowest, then pick one of those remaining. Depending on how busy they are, how good of a reputation they have, and even how enthused they are about your project, their estimated price will range from substantial to outrageous, so be prepared. Upholstery and trim work is somewhat specialized and not everyone has the patience or the mindset to do it, so if the price seems too high, just tell them you are getting some estimates and ideas on what to get done. If the price is within your budget, feel free to ask for some references so you can see samples of their work.

All professionals make their money by charging for their time, but in professions that use materials, they charge for that as well. Upholsterers, just like other contractors, usually mark up the price of the materials to make some additional money without raising their hourly rate. However, you may be able to walk in to the same supply house as they do and purchase upholstery material for the same low price.

I mention this not to tell you that your upholstery job is going to cost more, but instead to potentially save you some money and/or avoid hard feelings. If an upholsterer gives you an estimate of "xx dollars plus materials," you may get the idea that you could buy the material yourself and have your stitching done at a lower price. But it doesn't work that way. The upholsterer probably has a good idea of the amount of materials needed from your preliminary discussions, and therefore already has an amount of material markup to be added to his total bill. Depending on the upholsterer, the majority of their profit may be based on the time, or it may be based on the material. If the majority of their profit is based on material markup, you will greatly affect their profit margin by providing your own materials. This is not to say that all upholsterers will balk at you providing your own materials, but it is something that should be discussed and agreed upon early in the project.

## How good is their work?

Upholsterers, just like all professionals, usually have their customers swearing at them or swearing by them. When inquiring about a particular professional's work, ask more than one person and don't be afraid to read between the lines when someone gives their opinion. Some contractors are very good at what they do, but poor businesspeople. If you get this impression about an upholster you are considering, you will have to decide if the quality of their work offsets the possible headaches while working with them.

Sadly, some people are never happy with any service that they have to pay for, no matter how good of a job. They always think that they had to pay too much or the job took too long. Look at the work that was done for them and if it looks good and is within your budget, it will probably turn out okay. If this unhappy customer points out shoddy work (seams that aren't straight, ill-fitting seat covers, or other sloppy work), then listen to their advice about finding a different trimmer.

On the other hand, we all know that word of mouth is the best advertisement. If everyone who a potential contractor refers you to is well pleased and can show suitable examples of the upholsterer's work, that should tell you a lot. Of course, bear in mind that most people will not refer you to someone who is going to give them a less than sparkling review.

If you are located in an area that has an abundance of automotive trimmers, you may find that some cater more to restoration projects, while others specialize in street rods, trucks, or muscle cars. All things being equal (price, quality of work, reputation, etc.) choose the person who specializes in the type of vehicle you have. Not that one of the other upholsterers couldn't do just as good a job, but they may run into minor difficulties particular to your style of vehicle. Additionally, they may have preconceived notions about how something should be done that may differ from what you want.

### YOURSELF

What if you live in Deadatnight, Iowa, and there aren't any upholsterers within a day's drive? Or more realistically, you don't have the budget to pay for a "professional" trim job? Upholstery work is not something that can be done by just anyone, but if you have the mindset for it, and the time and patience, you can do a lot of the work yourself. Everyone who is now an experienced upholsterer at one time was not. Since this is complicated and time-consuming work, start small and work your way into it in steps before attempting to reupholster an entire vehicle. Depending on the scope of the project, you may be able to enroll in a continuing education course at a local technical school or community college and use part of your upholstery job as homework. You would not be the first person to recover a car seat through this approach.

## You can start now

Now before you relocate the wife's Singer to the garage, realize that automotive upholstery work requires an industrial-quality sewing machine. Barring that minor setback, you can start on the upholstery of your dreams right now.

Some, but not all, upholstery tasks can be completed without a sewing machine.

Depending on the vehicle, door panels can be repainted to look brand new using the same or a different color. Or, they can be completely covered with tweed or vinyl using various adhesives. Many pickup trucks from the 1950s through 1970s have a small panel attached to the inside of the roof, rather than a traditional headliner. Like door panels, a panel like this can be redone without the need for a sewing machine.

New carpet can also be installed without sewing; however, depending on the contour of your vehicle's floor, it may need several different pieces to fit correctly. You may be able to work around this with judicious use of Velcro.

An ever-expanding aftermarket makes reupholstering your vehicle a much easier task for the do-it-yourselfer. Several companies offer seat covers, carpet kits, dash pads, and replacement door panels for most muscle cars from the 1960s and 1970s (refer to the appendix for a partial list). The list of available upholstery kits grows all the time, so do some research for what may be available for your particular vehicle. The potential drawback for many of these products is that they must be limited (at least somewhat) to stock (non-modified) configurations.

## Do you have the time to devote to the project?

As an amateur, it will most likely take you longer to complete the upholstery than a trained professional who does this work every day. Even so, doing the work yourself may be more convenient than being without the vehicle in question for a week or two. You won't be able to utilize the vehicle while it is being reupholstered by a professional; however, you can still drive the car to work or school during the week if you work on it on the weekends. It may take you several weekends to get everything finished, but if you break down the job into manageable tasks, the weekend customizer can get a lot done.

With an available carpet kit and a set of custom seat covers, you should be able to replace the carpet and have new covers on the seats in a weekend or two. You can install new door panels in another weekend. Spend the next weekend detailing the dash, cleaning the windows, and perhaps installing a new stereo and your interior will look much better in less than a month.

A quick note about seat covers: their quality varies. The often overpriced, yet still cheap seat covers available at your local discount store are on the lower end of the spectrum. They are slipped on over the existing upholstery and are pretty much universal in fit—so they don't fit anything very well. On the other hand, upholstery kits from specialized

Oh, those ugly seat covers. The previous owner of this Chevrolet Beretta must have been a smoker. Even though the back seat looked okay, the seat covers on the front buckets could not hide cigarette burns, rips, and tears. The cheap seat covers covered everything but just didn't look good. These are the cheap, universal seat covers designed to fit high-back bucket seats, no matter what the make of the vehicle. "One size fits all" usually doesn't.

aftermarket sources often fit just like the original upholstery. The original upholstery is removed, and the new covers are slipped on and secured in place with hog rings or other suitable fastening mechanism. This latter option is similar to what you would be getting from an upholsterer, except that he or she would install them on the seats for you. The upholsterer doesn't run the seats themselves through a sewing machine; they make a seat cover (using the original cover as a pattern or measuring the seat itself), then install it on the seat.

## It will cost less, but will you get what you want?

It may be that you have found an upholsterer whose work you like, but their rate is a little (or maybe a lot) more than what you want to spend. You might very well be able to learn how to do the upholstery work yourself, but is that what you really want to do? If you have been laboring over a street rod or a muscle car restoration for the last couple of years, you don't want to (and shouldn't) drop the ball now, simply because the upholstery isn't done yet and you are running out of cash. If your thoughts of learning upholstery are simply to get this current vehicle done with and go no further, you should probably figure out a way to get a pro to do the job and save yourself the trouble. You will be happier with the end result in the long run if your heart is not into doing the work yourself. Finding a temporary part-time job for some extra cash may be less trouble and aggravation than botching the interior of your own car.

## Can you do the work?

On the other hand, if you like tinkering with automobiles, are particular about details, and have patience, learning how to do upholstery work may be a great way to save some money on your car project and make a few bucks on the side afterward. With any group of automobile enthusiasts, many of them do their own mechanical work. A smaller number of them do body and paintwork, but even less perform quality upholstery work. Look at your circle of friends, assess their talents, and then assess your own. If no one does upholstery work, you may have clients lined up already if you decide (and prove) that you can do the work they need to have done. You may not make a lot of money, but if you have a craft that you can trade for work on your ride, you have accomplished the same thing.

---

## FREQUENTLY ASKED QUESTIONS OF UPHOLSTERERS

For perspective on the upholstery process, I talked with Shawn Appleman of Appleman Interiors, in Lancaster, Ohio. Below are some of the questions his customers ask, and Shawn's answers.

***Does my car need to run?*** Yes! Early in my career, I would let unfinished cars into the shop so the owners would not miss their appointment. But problems cropped up when they had to remove our work again to make the vehicle run. After making a few long-distance phone calls to explain how to remove complex panels we had reupholstered, and then repairing the panels that got damaged in the process, we put a stop to this. It's extremely difficult to engineer custom panels around nonexistent items such as gas pedals, brake pedals, A/C and heater hoses, or to plan for a bundle of wires that will later be installed. We now have a checklist of items a car must have before it pulls into the shop. Although we never drive a customer's car, often it is important to move it around the shop to deliver other vehicles. Brakes need to be bled, steering must be hooked up, etc.

***Can I use wire loom for running my wires?*** No. Although it is a good way to hide unsightly wiring, wire loom is poor to use inside. It causes lumps under carpet and often gets in the way over kick panels. Behind panels, I recommend tightly bundling wires with wire ties (leaving extra slack in the wires where they will go above panels). On the floor, I need wires to be laid flat; side by side like a ribbon. Aluminum furnace tape works well to attach wires to the floor in this manner. If you have a stubborn spot where tape won't hold, use a craft hot glue gun. Apply the hot glue to the floor and then press the wires into it. Wait for it to cool and you have a great hold that keeps the wires tight to the floor, allowing jute pad to be applied smoothly.

***What seats should I use?*** This one depends on how you plan to use the vehicle. High-back bucket seats look goofy in a roadster and aluminum racing buckets are impractical in a cross-country cruiser. Comfort should be your first choice, followed by style. A stock tuck and rolled seat will look out of place in a slick hi-tech shoebox. But most of all, *never* settle. I've seen far too many late-model minivan bench seats in early pickup trucks that force the driver's knees into his chest.

***Will you mount the seats?*** No. All seats must be mounted with all their hardware in a position comfort-able to the owner. Personal preference should be taken into account. I enjoy sitting close to the floor in most hot rods (Ohio Low) and many customers have their own opinions. So it's best to mount your own seats ahead of time to get the best relationship between driver, steering wheel, pedals and the view through the windshield.

***Does the car need to be painted?*** Yes, yes, and well . . . yes. This question was never posed until a certain door panel company ran an ad stating you can do your inte-rior and then remove it before painting to avoid damage to paint. We do this for a living and take all precautions to prevent chips, scratches, and accidents when installing upholstery.

# CHAPTER 3
# TOOLS AND MATERIALS

## TOOLS

Except for an industrial-quality sewing machine, most of the tools required for upholstery work are readily available and relatively inexpensive when compared to other tools, such as for mechanics or auto body repair. Besides the sewing machine, the largest single expense most likely will be for an air compressor, and those are available in a multitude of sizes and prices. As with many professions, the list of necessary tools grows with each job performed. You may start with a pair of scissors, a tape measure, and a pair of hog ring pliers on your first upholstery job, but undoubtedly you will require different and more specialized tools as you gain more experience and work with different types of seats.

### Layout tools

Among the most basic, least expensive, and most easily located tools are those for measuring and layout. Although most upholstery material is cut larger than needed, slipped into place, and the excess trimmed, you will still need a tape measure to determine approximate measurements. Obviously, the material will need to be at least some certain dimension prior to trimming. An 8- or 12-foot tape measure should be plenty long for any automotive upholstery tasks. A 16-foot tape may be necessary if you are working on stretched limos, hearses, or sedan deliveries, but if you are doing those vehicles, you should probably buy an extra tape anyway as the larger tape will be cumbersome for smaller jobs. For some tasks, a carpenter's steel tape works best, while a dressmaker's cloth tape works better for others. Tape measures are inexpensive when you calculate the use-to-expense ratio, so buy a couple just in case you misplace one. Also realize that a cheap tape measure works just as well as an expensive one, and what can be wrong with a tape measure?

For laying out pleats or patterns, a yardstick or meter stick is necessary. The solid measuring stick holds its position easier than a flexible tape measure while trying to mark off even increments. Try to find a measuring stick with a metal edge so it can serve as a straightedge for cutting against when using a razor knife.

For marking pleats, reference marks, or simply the outline for where to cut, use chalk or a China marker. A China marker works best on vinyl or leather materials and can be cleaned off with 3M's General Purpose Adhesive Cleaner on a paper towel or soft cloth. Chalk works best on

These certainly are not all the tools an upholsterer uses, but this photo shows that most upholsterer's tools are simple. These tools are readily available and relatively inexpensive. Clockwise from the upper right are a pneumatic stapler, pliers, screwdriver, ice pick, utility knife, scissors (or shears), staple remover, and two lead weights.

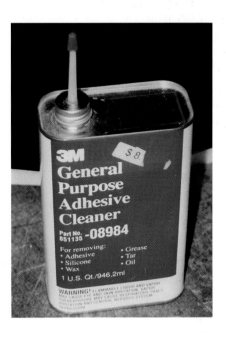

Anytime you work with upholstery materials and contact cement, have some 3M General Purpose Adhesive Cleaner on hand. Since most contact cement is applied by spray (whether from a spray gun or an aerosol can), there is the possibility of overspray. By applying some of this cleaner to a paper towel or soft cloth, you can remove contact cement overspray or reference marks from a China marker or chalk from vinyl or leather material.

tweed or cloth materials; however, you should avoid using chalk on vinyl or leather as the grit in the chalk can actually cut this material slightly. China markers can be found in larger art stores or photographic supply stores, while chalk is available at most art stores or anywhere school supplies are sold.

### Cutting tools

Upholstery revolves around cutting material into smaller pieces and then sewing or gluing them back together, so cutting tools are essential. Foam material can be cut with scissors if it is thin or with a razor knife if it is thick. If using a razor knife, cut against a metal straightedge to maintain a uniform edge. Use a metal or aluminum straightedge so that the razor knife does not cut into it and leave a non-straight edge. Much like for foam, scissors and razor knives work equally well for cutting fabric upholstery material.

Scissors work best when they are sharp, so use a high-quality pair that maintains its edge. Sharpening scissors yourself and avoiding cutting wire or staples are benefits. Any good upholsterer has at least two good pairs of scissors so that a freshly sharpened pair is always available.

When cutting certain types of insulation or thicker backing materials, use a razor knife. ABS door panels can usually be cut with a razor knife, while wood-based door panels may need to be cut with a wood cutting saw with the appropriate amount of teeth for the material. More teeth give a finer cut, but take longer. As long as you take your time and don't rush the process, most wood-based or ABS door panels can be cut using power jig or scroll saws. Relatively thin (⅛ inch or less) lauan wood paneling can be cut with a razor knife and is the desired method for some. If you are cutting pieces that need to have exact straight edges, it may be easier and less time consuming to use a razor knife along a metal straightedge than to draw a line to follow with a saw, and then have to follow that up with a file to achieve the required precision edge.

### Industrial sewing machine

A heavy-duty, industrial-quality sewing machine is necessary if you are sewing automotive-grade upholstery material. These can be found in advertisements in automotive publications or through your local upholstery supply store.

The standard machine most trimmers use today is a single-needle, dual-foot machine, with both forward and reverse sewing capabilities. Although a reverse feature is not an absolute necessity, it will make locking the beginning and ending of seams easier. This type of machine uses a full spool for the top thread and a smaller bobbin for the bottom thread. Two presser feet help keep the material

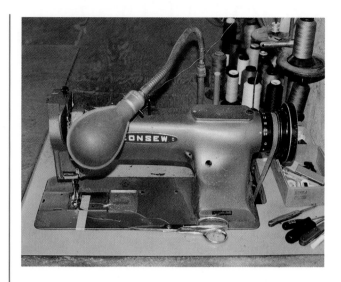

*This is what makes an upholsterer's world go around: an industrial-quality sewing machine. Several kits for do-it-yourselfers eliminate sewing, but if you are doing upholstery work on more than one vehicle, step up and buy a sewing machine. Different models are available, but the typical type used for automotive upholstery is a single-needle, dual-foot machine. The ability to sew in reverse is a plus, but not an absolute necessity.*

properly aligned while you sew. One is located beside the needle and is referred to as the sewing foot. A second foot located behind the needle is referred to as the dual feed foot. A serrated bar, called a feed dog, is located under the needle. In synchronization with the needle, it moves up under the fabric and pulls the fabric forward one stitch.

Some machines use a walking needle (or walking foot). This walking needle moves forward one stitch as it passes through the fabric, and in combination with the feed dog, pulls the fabric forward.

### Air compressor, spray gun, and pneumatic stapler

Air compressors can be used for a variety of tools, but for upholstery work they are used for a spray gun and a pneumatic stapler. If you are buying an air compressor, buy a larger capacity (albeit more expensive) model for other non-upholstery jobs. If this compressor will be dedicated to upholstery work, a relatively smaller (and less expensive unit) will work for a one- or two-person shop. If more than a couple of people will use air tools at one time, invest in a larger air compressor.

If you are using a stationary air compressor, consider the installation of a piping system with a water trap or air dryer located at the end. The water trap and air dryer are not as critical in upholstery work as they are to painters, but having dry air is beneficial to your pneumatic accessories. Even for home use, a small air supply system with ¾-inch to 1-inch pipe is advantageous. A copper or galvanized pipe running downhill away from a compressor toward a water trap or dryer allows moisture accumulations in heated air to flow away from the compressor and toward the trap or dryer. Since the hot air has time to cool inside pipes, moisture suspended in the air condenses into droplets that are captured and retained as a liquid in the trap.

You can run ¾- to 1-inch copper or galvanized pipe up from the compressor location to the ceiling, then attach a horizontal section to the riser and run it slightly downhill toward the opposite end of the garage or workshop. Another section then runs down the wall to a convenient point where a water trap or air dryer is mounted. Working air lines connect at the trap or dryer to be used for pneumatic tools or spray guns. In larger trim shops, air line drops from the main air supply line are located wherever necessary to be convenient for the air tool operator.

To keep portable air compressors mobile and prevent their operational vibration from causing damage to solid piping mounted to walls, connect your compressor to your piping system with a short, flexible air hose. By doing this, you can easily disconnect the air compressor from the piping system to move it for other kinds of jobs.

Rather than a heavy-duty air hose that is designed to be driven over and withstand other extreme shop conditions, a lighter weight, self-coiling air hose works fine for upholstery work. Depending on the size of your shop and if you have a stationary air compressor or a portable unit, it may be beneficial to have more than one air hose connection.

Unlike when purchasing a spray gun for applying paint or other refinish materials, an expensive spray gun is not recommended. You are using it to apply glue, so you don't need to spend the extra money for a top-of-the-line spray gun. It will need to be cleaned on a routine basis with the appropriate cleaner, but eventually it will need to be replaced. If you need a spray gun for applying paint or other refinish materials (such as to paint seat frames or coloring door panels), purchase a different spray gun.

## Fastening tools

After you have cut, sewn, glued, and done whatever else may be required to make a new seat cover or door panel, you will need to secure the material to the seat frame or door. Most but not all seat covers are secured in place with hog rings. These are similar to an extremely heavy-duty staple in that they go through the material to hold it in place. The difference is that hog ring pliers are used to close

the open end around a wire or rod in the seat frame, rather than flattening it out against itself.

In the early 1900s, many vehicles had wooden substructures to hold the body together. This wood made a logical attachment point for upholstery panels, so those panels were tacked in place with small nails or tacks. Magnetic tack hammers with a relatively small head (compared to a framing hammer) are used to hammer small tacks into wooden tack strips or these wooden substructures to hold the material in place. For the most part, tacks are no longer used, but you may encounter some that need to be removed if you are reupholstering a vehicle that was built in the early 1900s. The magnetic feature of these hammers is useful as most of these tacks are small. You can attach the tack to the magnetic hammer and then drive it in place, rather than attempt to hold the tack with your finger and thumb as with larger nails.

To remove and re-install seats, a variety of combination wrenches or ratchet and sockets is necessary. A variety of screwdrivers is required to remove and replace all the screws you may encounter, including Phillips, slotted, Torx, and other special fasteners. Each vehicle that you work on inevitably will cause you to purchase at least one more tool for your collection.

## Working space

Whenever you are doing upholstery work, you will need a large, flat table or workbench at a comfortable height. Whether you will sit or stand while working is for you to

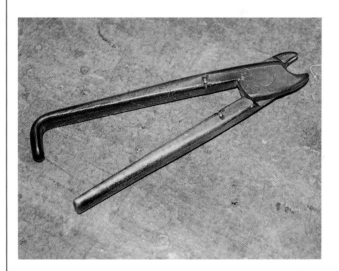

*These are straight hog ring pliers, although some trimmers prefer bent hog ring pliers. The bent type may be easier to use in tight situations but most upholsterers learn to use whichever type is available when they do their first trim work. The jaws are notched to hold the hog ring in place while the upholsterer positions the pliers and the material.*

decide, but the worktable should be at a comfortable height for both. Upholsterers often have their tables set at a comfortable height for standing, and then use a stool rather than a chair to sit at the same table. You may be able to sit some of the time, depending on the height of your table and the chair you are sitting at, but you will be standing more than you may expect at first. Since you are standing much of the time, you may want to invest in one of those work-station floor mats that reduce fatigue.

The size of the table should be large enough to roll out the largest piece of material that you may be working with. In most cases, this will be a headliner that may be 6 feet wide and, for some vehicles, close to 10 feet long. You won't need all this table space all the time, but when you do need it, you will be glad you have it. Your worktable should be covered with thin cardboard or Masonite to provide a smooth surface, yet it should be inexpensive enough so that it can be replaced without spending a fortune when it begins showing excessive wear.

Since the size of the table will leave a substantial footprint in your shop, use the area below as storage. You can store rolls of material at one end and other accessories such as nuts, bolts, and seat hardware in storage bins under the other end. How much storage space you require depends partially on how you run your business. If you finish all of one job before starting another, you will not need room to store additional seats and their related hardware. If, on the other hand, customers drop off their stuff "so you'll have it when you are ready for it," you will need significantly more storage area.

## Other tools

Pliers, wire cutters, ice picks, and small weights are also necessary. Pliers and wire cutters help to remove old wires, hog rings, and nails securing old upholstery. Ice picks, awls, or other similar lineup devices align multi-layer door panels during their construction. An ice pick or awl is also useful for poking a small hole in carpet when searching for seat or seatbelt mounting holes. Small weights such as chunks of lead or bean bags are sometimes necessary to hold material to a panel while the contact adhesive dries, or to hold material out of the way when applying adhesive. Whatever you use for weight, make sure that it is reasonably soft and has no sharp edges.

Other tools that may be required as your trimming experience grows include heat guns, specialized clip removal tools, and paint equipment. Heat guns are used to soften material to smooth out wrinkles or to remove glued-on emblems from door panels or other interior panels. Make sure that you do not concentrate too much heat in one place

anytime that you are using a heat gun as you quickly may do more harm than good. The automotive industry uses several different types of retaining clips that are almost impossible to remove unless you have the right tool. With that special tool, they are removed quite easily, making it good sense to spend the few bucks necessary to purchase it rather than to drive yourself crazy making do without.

Do yourself a favor anytime you start an upholstery project and see if the vehicle requires any special tools. Factor the price of the tool in with expenses for the job. If you are painting any interior pieces that require something other than what is available in a simple spray can, you will need a paint spray gun. You won't need to spend the money on the highest quality guns like those that are used for automobile painting, but a high-quality spray gun with air and fluid adjustments will come in handy at times.

## MATERIALS

### Padding material

Three types of foam are commonly used as padding material: molded, open cell, and closed cell. Seats for many late-model vehicles are made with molded foam. This is foam injected into a mold of the desired shape. When the molding process is completed, the foam is the correct shape and size of the seat. It is then attached to a framework and upholstered with the desired material. This type of foam is dense and provides firm support while maintaining its shape.

Open-cell foam is the material most commonly associated with automotive upholstery. It comes in rolls, is available in various thickness, and is fairly soft. It can be cut easily with a sharp razor knife and can be glued together to form different shapes. A common example is a raised bolster around the front (and sometimes edges) of a seat or around a seat back. Open-cell foam usually is sandwiched between the seat frame and the seat upholstery.

Closed-cell foam is much like molded foam in density, yet comes in rolls and is available in different thickness. A common example of closed-cell foam is disposable drinking cups. Closed-cell foam is most commonly used as padding in door panels or in headliners, and especially with sculptured patterns. Closed-cell foam can be glued with contact cement into many layers, providing a three-dimensional effect. Vinyl or tweed material can then be glued to the foam to form truly custom panels. About the only drawback to making a sculptured panel using this method is that the pattern should avoid tiny, intricate shapes. Instead, use larger, more sweeping shapes so that the upholstery material can be more easily worked into the crevices of the pattern.

Whether you use open-cell or closed-cell foam, it must have a backing if you are going to sew material directly to it. You must either use scrim-backed foam or attach your own backing to keep the thread from pulling through it. Scrim-backed foam has a layer of material that loosely resembles screen door wire attached to it. If you don't have scrim-backed foam, glue a layer of muslin to the back of the material to serve the same purpose.

## Seat coverings

Seats can be covered in just about any kind of material; however, some materials look better than others. On a period-perfect, nostalgic hot rod roadster, an Indian or Mexican blanket with the excess folded nicely and hog ringed to the seat frame looks just as appropriate as the finest leather looks on a fully restored Rolls-Royce. Often, cost-conscious rodders will attempt to be nostalgic by throwing a blanket over an otherwise barren seat. Without taking the time and effort to secure the blanket to the seat, it ends up looking more like an unmade bed. No matter what material you use for upholstery, do the work neatly. You'll be prouder of it, and it will serve you longer.

Although the material used for the upholstery should be on par with the materials and workmanship on the rest of the vehicle, there is a wide price range on seat upholstery materials. The following prices no doubt will become outdated during the life of this book, but they are current as of its writing and are all from the same source, so they serve as comparable examples. Unless noted otherwise, all materials listed are 54 inches wide. Allante vinyl, a high-quality alternative to leather with excellent durability that comes in a variety of colors, retails for $20 per yard—that is, a 3-foot-long piece that is 54-inches wide. Tweed upholstery material that is similar to wool runs $20 to $30 per yard, depending on the color selected. Tweed material probably has the widest selection of colors from which to choose. Ultraleather HP, a manmade leather-like material, costs just under $100 per yard. It is as durable as leather, somewhat softer, and slightly less expensive. Ultrasuede HP will set you back close to $150 per yard. For real leather material, expect to pay $8 to $12 per square foot. Leather is not sold by the same yard measurement as the other materials because hide sizes vary.

When purchasing material, each yard is 3 feet long by width of the material. In the preceding examples, the rolls were 54 inches wide. Obviously, a yard of 48-inch-wide material would provide less material than a yard of 60- or 72-inch-wide material. To help give an accurate comparison between the prices of leather priced per square foot and those priced per yard, a yard of 54-inch-wide material provides 13.5 square feet. A square yard is the same as 9 square feet. This information all boils down to the fact that

This is just a portion of one upholstery vendor's exhibit at a large hot rod event. Most upholstery suppliers will have samples of their materials. At an event like this, you could purchase individual samples to take home and mull over. If you are doing upholstery for others, you will need to purchase sample displays from which your customers can choose their material.

a yard of vinyl or inexpensive tweed costs about $20, while the same amount of leather costs $108 to $162. Quite a difference by the time you figure how much material will be required to upholster a vehicle, yet a significant difference in the finished product as well.

In addition to costs, leather has another drawback. Manmade material comes in exact widths by whatever length is needed. Real leather comes in the shape of the animal, be it cow, ostrich, or snakeskin. These odd shapes of animal skins can end up with lots of waste (and therefore lots of expense) if you do not take their shape into consideration and plan the patterns of your interior carefully.

How much you choose to spend on material is up to you. If you are recovering the seats in a daily driver that has more miles than you care to remember and could use an engine rebuild, you probably will be happy with new vinyl seat covers. There is nothing wrong with the high-quality vinyl materials that are available today. When not abused, they provide years of good service. On the other hand, if you are building a one-off, custom vehicle to

 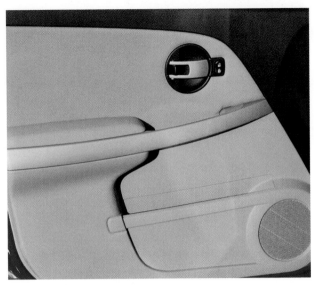

*Above left: If you are restoring a vehicle such as this 1960s Chevrolet station wagon, you can find replacement or new old stock door panels like the one shown. This panel consists of a piece of cardboard covered with one piece of vinyl secured in place with staples on the back side. The armrest is attached to the door panel with screws or bolts prior to installation on the door. Small clips or screws hold the door panel in place, while the door handle and window riser slide onto their respective mechanisms and are held in place with a spring-loaded clip. If desired, you could duplicate this type of door panel with nicer material. Above right: This is a type of modular door panel covered with different materials. The entire door panel is made up of multiple pieces that are each covered in their own material (different colors, different fabrics, etc.) before the door panel is reassembled to become one piece.*

prove that money is no problem for you, a leather or leather alternative will show that extra bit of style, comfort, and elegance. Quite honestly, with the high quality of today's upholstery materials, many people can't tell the difference between vinyl and leather. A true leather interior has a distinctive aroma; however, you could put a baseball glove and a pair of cowboy boots under the seat to give your vinyl-clad interior that leather smell. Don't laugh, it has been done.

### Door panels

Door panels usually are covered in the same material as the seats, if they are covered. For many vehicles manufactured between the 1960s and the 1990s, door panels were formed plastic painted to match the upholstery. Paint for refinishing these un-upholstered panels can be purchased at a local automotive paint and supply store.

### Floor coverings

In very early automobiles, the floor was made of wood and had no covering, except possibly for some paint or varnish. As sheet metal came into common use as a floor material, rubber mats became the common covering. These were relatively cheap, easy to cut to the correct size, and provided suitable traction while entering or exiting the vehicle.

Postwar cars began the current use of carpet to cover the floor. Carpet in its various blends of materials is still the most common automotive floor covering, but there are others. Although its use as a floor covering is usually associated with custom-built vehicles, leather and often exotic leather (such as stingray, ostrich, and alligator) are becoming common.

### Headliner material

Material for the headliner usually is the same as whatever is used for the seats and door panels. The headliner is not in our normal line of sight while in a vehicle, and as such has not proven to be a place for straying away from the norm (at least not with regard to the material being used). One notable exception I saw in a hot rod several years ago was the backboard from a pinball machine in the place of a headliner.

Although the headliner material is often the same as that used for the seats and the door panels, you do need to take into consideration the material's weight. The headliner is affected more by gravity than it will ever be from wear and tear. For this reason, it makes good sense to use material that is lighter in weight than similar material that would be better suited for seats, door panels, and other high-traffic areas.

# CHAPTER 4
# INSULATION

**A**utomotive insulation can be one of two types and may work as both types to a certain extent. The first type maintains a comfortable temperature inside compared to the extremes of heat or cold outside. Its use maximizes the effects and minimizes the workload of the automobile's heater and air conditioning systems.

A second type of insulation absorbs and damps unwanted sound. This works toward minimizing annoying engine and road noise inherent to all automobiles. By reducing extraneous noises, the insulation allows you to hear your stereo system or other audio communication equipment more clearly. It allows you to talk to other people in the vehicle without screaming.

## CLIMATE CONTROL

Whether your vehicle's body is made of steel, aluminum, fiberglass, carbon fiber, or something else, that material alone will do little to shield occupants from the ambient temperature outside the vehicle. If the sun beats down on a metal box, the inside gets very warm, very fast. If the box has an air conditioning system, the inside will be cooler, but the A/C unit will work much harder than necessary just to keep up. Likewise, a heater warms up the inside of that steel box on a cold day, but the heat quickly will find its way out of that uninsulated box. Just like your home, vehicles need insulation to keep the driver and passengers comfortable on all but that perfect day, meant just for cruising.

Early on, automotive designers realized this and began putting insulation material in relatively small amounts in vehicles. This material (usually jute felt) was found under the carpet or floor mats. On some higher priced vehicles, it could be found between the layers of the hood and the trunk lid.

Today's vehicles have more insulation in them than ones made years ago, but there is usually room for more. If you are rebuilding a vehicle, what may have been an adequate amount of insulation in the vehicle originally may need to be replaced. Although some insulation materials may seem expensive at first, their use will improve your driving experience, which is a bargain at most any price.

In their search for improved insulation, automotive engineers have borrowed from other disciplines. Reflective heat shields that the aerospace industry has developed work well in automobiles. This material, usually consisting of highly reflective aluminum, shields occupants and heat-

*Beneath the trunk floor mat of this Chevrolet Beretta is jute felt insulation material. This material was originally made from natural jute fibers from Indonesia, but a petrochemical substitute is now available. Until relatively recent developments in man-made insulating material, jute felt was considered to be the best material for heat and noise insulation.*

sensitive equipment such as computer systems from high temperatures produced by the exhaust and other systems.

Engineers have also developed materials that bond the heat reflective surface of aluminum to a fibrous padding. In addition to reflecting heat away from the surface, the padding material absorbs and dampens noise, providing some sound-deadening advantages.

These damper/reflective barrier combinations are available at automotive shops that sell interior products or at large home building supply centers. The material is sold in prepackaged rolls from automotive shops or in bulk from home improvement centers. It comes in various widths and is easily cut with scissors or a utility knife.

For use on floor surfaces, remove the carpet and floor mats, cut the insulation material to size, and slip it into place. Although reinstalling the carpet or floor mats will hold the insulation in place, spraying some contact cement onto the insulation material and the floor prior to installation will not hurt anything. On vertical surfaces or on the inside of the roof, a spray adhesive such as 3M's Top and Trim Adhesive is necessary to hold the insulation material in place. This is a contact cement, so the adhesive must be applied to both surfaces, allowed to become tacky, and

*Reflective heat barrier insulation is being used in the roof of this Ford Model A pickup truck. Purchased in rolls (various widths are available), this material can be cut to the desired size and shape with scissors or a utility knife. It is secured to the roof between roof supports. This insulation material can be used on horizontal or vertical surfaces, but must be glued with contact cement. The cement is applied to both mating surfaces and allowed to dry to the point of being tacky before the pieces are joined. If the contact cement is not allowed to "tack up," it will not hold as well as intended.*

pushed into place. Be sure to use a contact cement that is permanent or the insulation material from your ceiling may soon be in your lap. Use aluminum-faced tape or duct tape to cover any seams. Car tops get very hot while in the summer sun, so adhesive used to apply insulation material to the inside of a car roof should be rated as "high temperature." This adhesive should have a rating of at least 160 degrees Fahrenheit.

Insulation material alone will not help if there are significant air leaks in the vehicle's cabin structure. You must eliminate holes in the body, which should be repaired by welding in patch panels or replacing body panels if the holes are significant. Apart from rust-prone areas, holes are most commonly found in the firewall where electrical wires or heater hoses enter the passenger cabin from the engine compartment. On older vehicles, previous owners may have added holes, some of which may no longer be needed. If all holes are needed but have excessive clearance around them, use foam to seal the gap. Incomplete welds or missing seam sealer also allows air leaks. If this is the case, purchase seam sealer (an automotive caulking) at an automotive paint and supply store and apply. Collision damage that has not been repaired properly (or completely) also allows air leaks and may possibly cause noise problems.

You may also need to replace weather stripping around doors and windows. Replacement weather stripping can be purchased in kits for some vehicles or in bulk for most vehicles. If you need to replace weather stripping around your doors, run a piece of tape or draw a line around it to indicate proper placement prior to removing it. You can now pull the old weather stripping off, using a putty knife if necessary to loosen hard to remove areas.

Fit the new weather stripping around the door to check for length and also to verify that the placement between the door and the body is correct. Now apply a bead of weather strip adhesive (sometimes referred to as "gorilla snot") to the back side of the weather stripping per the instructions. Some brands need to become tacky, while others don't. Place the weather stripping into position and allow to dry before driving the vehicle. Many body shops use strips of masking tape to hold the weather strip in place while it sets up. Wipe away any excess adhesive and you are done.

## IMPROVED ACOUSTICS

As a car or truck operates, it generates noise. This noise is a result of the energy being transferred throughout the vehicle, creating a vibration. The body components such as the doors, floor, and roof act as a sounding board to transform this vibration into audible noise.

Years ago, the insulation material found beneath the carpet in vehicles was about all there was to deaden noise. Contemporary automotive design includes measures to improve the sound system by using acoustic material throughout the vehicle: from the engine compartment to minimize drivetrain noise; from the passenger cabin to minimize wind and road noise; and from the trunk compartment to minimize road and exhaust noise. These materials can also help prevent unwanted heat or cold from entering the passenger compartment. Ideally, the passenger

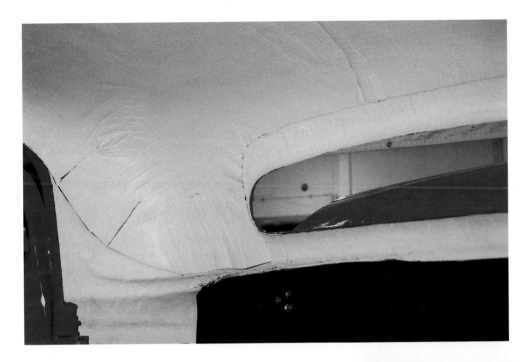

Anytime you are fortunate enough to have the bare hulk of a vehicle to deal with, sound deadening and thermal insulation should be added, such as in the roof of this hot rod coupe. The roof will not need to be insulated as much for sound as it will to keep out the sun's heat and keep in the air conditioner's cold air.

compartment would be a soundproof box. For the best results, a reflective heat-barrier-type insulation should be used in conjunction with a sound deadening insulation.

Sound deadening can be accomplished in one of two ways; damping or absorbing. Damping is the reduction of vibration and noise generated by resonant vibration in areas such as body panels, door panels, floorpans, and roof panels. Damping material should be at least one-half the thickness of the material to which it is being applied and cover approximately one-third to one-half of the surface area. The most effective material used in damping is a self-adhesive rubberized asphalt material that is acoustically "dead" because of its dense mass and weight, about 2 pounds per square foot. The best automotive dampers are water repellant.

Absorbers are materials that soak up sound and prevent sound waves from reflecting. Absorbers consist of dense fibrous materials with open pores. Open-cell foams and fiberglass are examples of sound-absorbing materials. Thick materials absorb low to high frequencies, while thin materials mainly absorb medium to high frequencies.

Material such as Dynamat is available to improve the sound quality in our automobiles. Dynamat is a thin, flexible, easy-to-cut-and-mold sheet that stops noise-causing resonance and vibration. This type of sound-deadening material can be applied to a specific panel to minimize its resonance, or it can be applied to an entire surface area to create a sound barrier and thermal insulator. Applying Dynamat to the inside of the doors only can make a noticeable reduction (3 to 6 decibels) of road noise. Covering the

The floor on this same hot rod can be well served with both damping- and absorber-type sound-deadening material. Closest to the floor is the absorber material that soaks up the sound from the drivetrain and the road. The next layer (partially pulled up in the photo) is the damping material that reduces vibrations that cause unwanted noise.

trunk and roof will further reduce the amount of road noise inside the vehicle.

Four grades of Dynamat make it suitable for a variety of applications and budgets. For the best compromise between cost and damping efficiency, Dynamat Original is available. It is suitable for most locations (floors, doors, side panels, and trunk floors), except where it would be installed upside down such as car roofs. Any of the other three grades would be suitable for that particular application. Dynamat Original requires a heat gun for application.

*continued on page 46*

# INSTALLING SOUND DEADENING MATERIAL

INSULATION

Before installing Dynamat, clean the area with a quick drying, residue-free solvent such as wax and grease remover found at an automotive paint and supply store. Spray or wipe the cleaner on with a clean towel, then wipe it off with a second towel to clean the surface thoroughly and ensure a permanent bond between the surface and the Dynamat.

Make a cardboard or paper template for the size and shape of the Dynamat to be installed. Use a utility knife or scissors to cut the Dynamat sheet to the correct size and shape. Remove the blue release liner from the back of the Dynamat and apply the Dynamat to the prepared surface. On large surfaces, remove the release liner in sections, working your way down and across the panel. To install Dynamat onto vertical surfaces or upside down, use an upholstery adhesive, such as 3M's Top and Trim Adhesive. This is a contact cement that should be applied to both surfaces for best results.

Use a small roller to work the Dynamat into all the contours of the metal panel. If any air pockets form, slit them with a utility knife and work the air out with the roller.

After the Dynamat is in place, install a layer of reflective heat-barrier-type insulation. You can use cardboard or Kraft paper to make patterns, then cut the material with a pair of sharp scissors. With the reflective insulation in place, use aluminized tape or duct tape to cover the seams.

*As seen in this photo, it is not necessary to completely cover the surface. Photos courtesy of Quiet Ride Solutions*

**2**

Dynamat materials can be installed in areas other than the passenger cabin to minimize heat and noise. Install it in the trunk using the same procedures as elsewhere.

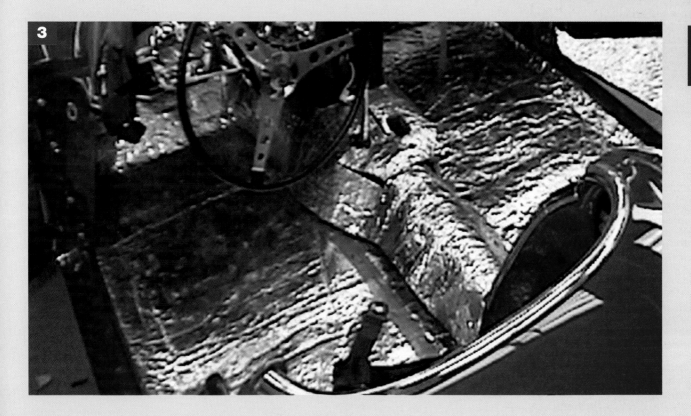

**3**

To maximize efficiency, install a layer of heat-barrier-type insulation. Use cardboard or Kraft paper to make patterns.

*continued from page 43*

Considered to be four times better than the original and at half the weight, Dynamat Xtreme is primarily used where heat is a factor such as on the floor or firewall. For hard-to-reach areas such as outer door skins or inner fender wells, Dynashield (liquid Dynamat) is recommended. Being a liquid, it must be sprayed on, taking 48 hours to cure. More suitable for racing applications, due to its extremely light weight, is Dynaplate. Three layers of Dynaplate is stronger than average car sheet metal. Two layers damp better than Dynamat Xtreme and weighs 32 percent less.

Any surface that you have access to is a good candidate for installing Dynamat; however, for best results, it should be applied to the insides of the doors, trunk, and floor areas first. If you choose to install more, it should then be applied to the interior panels of the rear deck, roof, hood, and then the fenders.

When installing any sort of insulation material in a vertical panel, such as the inside of a door or quarter panel, don't let the insulation material extend all the way to the lowest point of the cavity. The insulation material could soak up any moisture that enters into this area (such as rainwater or spilled liquid) and become an origin point for rust.

Another popular type of insulation is LizardSkin Ceramic Insulation. This product is more suitable for specially constructed vehicles (during the building process) or complete rebuilds that have been gutted on the interior. The liquid coating can be applied to a vehicle that is already finished; however, the extensive disassembly and masking required may prove to be impractical for some applications.

LizardSkin Ceramic Insulation is a water-based composition of air-filled ceramic and silica particles. These are combined with acrylic binders, making it similar to paint products in consistency. LizardSkin Ceramic Insulation claims to reduce engine and solar heat transfer by 25 to 30 degrees or more. It also serves to reduce noise by as much as 10 to 12 decibels.

Since LizardSkin Ceramic Insulation is a liquid, it can be applied to any clean and dry primed or painted rust-free surface. It can be brushed, sprayed, or even rolled on. Prior to application, mask off the areas that are not to be coated. Masking paper or masking film can be purchased at a local automotive paint and body supply store. Ambient temperatures must be 70 degrees Fahrenheit (21 degrees Celsius) or above. LizardSkin Ceramic Insulation should be applied in thin coats (0.010 to 0.015 inch), and will require three or four coats to achieve the desired thickness of 0.040 to 0.060 inch (about the thickness of a credit card). LizardSkin Ceramic Insulation must be allowed to dry fully to the touch between coats (dry finish will be flat/dull). Curing time before sanding or addi-

tional finishing is 24 hours at 70 degrees Fahrenheit (21 degrees Celsius) or warmer.

## SPRAY-ON UNDERCOATING

Another type of insulating material readily available at many auto parts stores is spray-on undercoating. This comes in aerosol cans and can be installed with relative ease. Although the heavy-duty version of this stuff isn't as common on the bottom of new vehicles as it used to be, spraying it inside of doors and fenders can help to minimize unwanted road noise and exhaust noise.

To spray this material inside of doors, make sure the windows are all the way up, then remove the interior door panel. The size of the door and window mechanism access holes varies from one vehicle to another; however, you should be able to spray most of the inside of the exterior door skin by directing the spray through these access holes. Spray approximately a ⅛-inch layer of the undercoating. Thicker coatings may leave residue on the door glass as it moves up and down.

Avoid getting any of the spray undercoating on the interior of the door or on the window riser mechanism. On metal parts, the undercoating can be removed by rubbing the part with a cloth soaked with a bit of kerosene.

Spray-on undercoating also can be applied to the inside of fenders. To spray the inside of the rear fenders, remove the trunk lining, if there is one. This is easy to do on most vehicles as the trunk lining material, at one extreme, lies there or, at the other extreme, may be held in place with plastic bolt-like fasteners. With the plastic fasteners, you can remove them by turning them counterclockwise. Remove the fasteners and pull the trunk lining out of the way. Like the bare door panels, the fenders have access holes. Apply the undercoating in layers up to about ⅛-inch thick. It isn't necessary to let the undercoating "dry" like paint material; however, you may choose to leave the trunk lining off until you are finished with all your undercoating application throughout the vehicle. This allows you to see if you missed any spots and won't hurt the undercoating as it firms up. When you are finished, reinstall and secure the trunk lining as it was previously.

Front fenders usually don't have any sort of lining in front of them, yet there may be other obstacles to contend with, such as a battery, windshield washer reservoir, or a myriad other engine-related items. The choice of which obstacles can be removed easily and which ones are not worth the trouble varies with each vehicle and is up to the person applying the undercoating. For this purpose, some undercoating products have a flexible hose attached to the nozzle that makes application somewhat easier.

INSULATION

# CHAPTER 5
## SEATING

Ideally, the only reason that you consider recovering your seats is that you want a different color or type of material. If this is the situation, you or the upholsterer could carefully remove the existing covers and use them as a pattern for the new material. The new material would be cut out, sewn together just like the originals, hog-ringed in place and presto, you are done. Chances are, however, that springs need repair, foam needs to be replaced, or the cover material is stretched so badly or torn beyond use as a pattern. Don't despair. None of those situations is new and they have all been remedied by more than one upholsterer.

The following sections break down the steps required to reupholster a seat, but the general procedure is as follows. Remove the seat(s) from the vehicle; remove the existing covers; assess the condition of the seat frame, springs, and cushions; make repairs as necessary; cut out and sew together the new cover; install and secure the cover; reinstall the seat in the vehicle.

### CHOOSING SEATS TO USE

If you are going to the time, trouble, and expense of reupholstering your vehicle's seats, you should also ask yourself if you really want to use the same seats. Not that there is anything wrong with using the existing seat, but if you are going to change seats, now is the time to make that decision. If the vehicle is in good condition otherwise and no additional modifications are in the plans, it would make sense simply to recover the existing seat to repair minor damage such as cigarette burns, small tears, or stains. On the other hand, if the seat is badly damaged to the point that portions of foam are missing or the seat frame itself is damaged, a replacement seat may be in order. If the frame is useable but has missing foam, new foam can be added to restore the seat prior to recovering it. Depending on the vehicle, a salvage yard may have a seat in much better condition that would be a direct bolt-in. It may still need to be reupholstered, but being structurally sound may be a better place to start. A salvage yard may have an optional seat for your model with more features, as well.

Your upholstery shop may be able to help you with your decision whether to replace or rebuild your existing seats, particularly if they have expertise with your model vehicle. The important thing is to get the seat you want, one that is structurally sound and meets your demands for

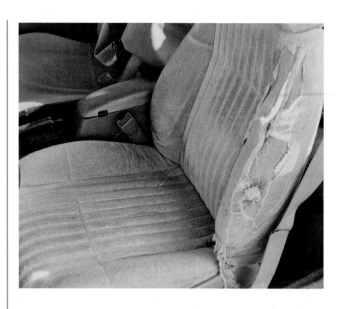

These seats are typical of what is often found beneath cheap seat covers. These particular seats are structurally sound and the foam needs only some minor repairs. The material covering the seats looks pretty bad, however, with large tears, various stains, lots of wear on the driver seat, and some cigarette burns. New upholstery would greatly improve the look of this vehicle.

comfort—or for originality. In a stock show car, you wouldn't want to fit a seat that differed in any way from what the car came with initially. Keep in mind, particularly on a vehicle with a long and checkered history, that the seats in the car when you got it might not be the correct ones. You wouldn't want to spend the money to redo a pair of bucket seats for your classic Jaguar only to learn later that it had Alfa Romeo seats in it.

If originality is not a concern, you also will choose the seat configuration. You can choose from bucket seats, bench seats, or split-back bench seats, which are a combination of the previous. You also have the choice of low backs, high backs, reclining, power seats, heated seats, or swivel seats. Of course, the larger the vehicle and how many seats you have has a direct impact on the number of seating configurations. This versatility is something that auto manufacturers are advertising heavily in their ads for minivans and SUVs.

When choosing seats, consider any effect particular configurations may have on ease of getting in and out of the vehicle. Seats typically found in sports cars or racing vehicles tend to have bolsters around the sides of the seat

*These seats are from an ordinary compact car. They have been reupholstered to suit the needs of this street rod. Starting with seat frames that are in good condition, repair or replace foam as necessary; then make and install new covers, and these seats look like new.*

*This seat was custom-made by the upholsterer for this particular vehicle. Often, this can be done by starting with a seat frame that is the correct width or cutting down one that is too wide. New foam padding can be installed and shaped to fit the vehicle before the upholstery goes on.*

and the seat back. The bolsters (along with seatbelts) help support your body as you twist and turn around a road course or down a canyon highway. They also project a competition image. Features developed for fast driving may not suit riders who are less agile and have difficulty entering and exiting a vehicle. A tight cockpit or wide running boards to step over compound this problem. Yet, with a skilled upholsterer, you needn't settle for all or nothing. If the vehicle has a competition heritage but a driver or passenger who would benefit from a little more wiggle room, the shop may be able to trim down the bolsters.

This split-back bench seat is from one of the many vendors that manufacture new seat frames for the automotive aftermarket. With small bolsters at the lower sides of the back, this seat gives the comfort of bucket seats, yet offers a bit more room than full buckets. The seat backs also fold forward to allow convenient access to some storage behind the seats.

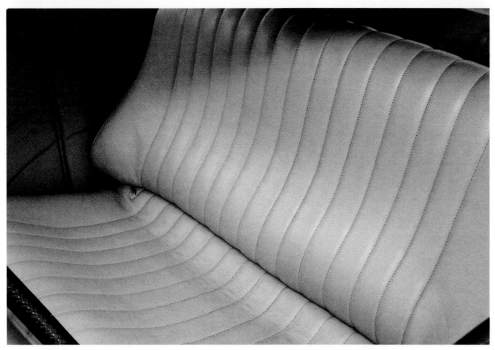

This seat is simply a bench seat, although it is in a street rod. Especially when doing pleats like these on the seat cushion and seat back, you should be very careful that they line up. These are aligned but may not appear to be because of the camera angle. There are seats out there where the pleats do not align, which makes the upholstery job look bad, as though the owner combined parts from different seats.

For the family sedan, a bench type seat would probably be more appropriate. A bench seat could have bolsters, but a bench seat is typically flatter. The flatter seat is easier to slide across to make room for the rest of the family or the family dog. A flatter seat is also more useful when hauling groceries, moving a television, or while on that perfect date.

## Original

If you are restoring a vehicle to stock condition, you will need to use the same type of seats that originally came with or at least were available with the vehicle. (However, nothing says that you have to use the very seats that were in it when you got it.) People who are adamant about

Seat backs that fold down are becoming more common on contemporary vehicles. A recent improvement on this concept is divided seat backs whose sections can fold down independently, allowing for the necessary combination of passengers and cargo.

This seat is typical of something that could be found at a swap meet or in a salvage yard. Although the cover is in better condition than many seats we've seen, it would most likely be reupholstered before being installed in a car. When searching for seats, the main thing to look for is that the seat is structurally sound; it also must fit your vehicle and needs.

Mild bolsters and a headrest in the front seats of this late-model SUV provide ample support and are comfortable; however, the material could be a little nicer. The two levers on the side are to adjust the seat. Seat height is adjusted with the front lever: it ratchets up to raise the seat or down to lower it. Seat back tilt is adjusted with the rear lever.

restoration will frequent swap meets, automotive Internet sites, and search in *Hemmings Motor News* to find just the right seats for their ride.

For many popular vehicles, aftermarket companies manufacture seat covers that are suitable replacements for originals. Unlike the universal seat covers found in discount stores, these seat covers are designed to fit very specific applications. The main difference between the cost of these covers and a custom trim job is that the consumer, rather than the upholsterer, installs the covers.

*Above: This seat is available from the aftermarket in an uncovered version. This display seat is covered to show a possible pattern, to display fabric available from this particular vendor, and to show that the seat is comfortable to sit in. Right: Same seat, same vendor, different material and pattern, giving an entirely different look. Note that this seat has a headrest installed as well.*

*Some companies prefer to sell uncovered seats and the upholstery material to their customers, while other companies (often displaying at the same events) manufacture their seat frames and cover them themselves so that they are ready to bolt-in upon delivery. Although the prices for brand-new seats may seem high, it may be a less expensive route than buying a new seat frame, the material, and paying someone else to cover it.*

## Aftermarket

If you are not "restoring" a vehicle and simply want new seats (for any reason) the contemporary aftermarket probably has you covered, so to speak. Aftermarket seats are available for most any vehicle from full-on racing Porsches to an otherwise stock Ford Contour. You can choose from completely upholstered, ready to bolt-in split-back bench seats covered in the finest leather to bare seat frames that you add foam to and upholster yourself.

When selecting any seat (aftermarket or salvage yard) that is not specifically designed for your vehicle, verify that the desired seat actually will fit inside of your vehicle. Most vehicles manufactured in the 1920s and 1930s were narrower than those manufactured after World War II. Automobiles were at their widest during the 1960s and 1970s, and then began decreasing in size again. The downsized vehicles of today still are larger than their counterparts from the early 1900s.

## REMOVING SEATS FROM THE VEHICLE

Seats (or their adjustment sliders) are usually held in place with four bolts that pass through the floorboard and into a threaded insert or nut welded to the underside of the floorpan. The threaded insert or nut being welded to the floorpan allows you to remove (or reinstall) the seats without a second person crawling beneath the vehicle to hold a wrench. If the nut is turning while you loosen the seat mounting bolts, re-weld the nut to the floorpan.

When removing the seats, make some notes to yourself as to how they are secured to the vehicle and what size bolts go where. You may think that you will remember (maybe you will), but by the time you get your seats back from the upholsterer, the reassembly may not be quite so clear in your mind. Basic seats won't pose too much of a problem; however, power or heated seats involve some wiring connections. Some photographs or detailed notes would be a good idea for reference when making these electrical connections.

With the seats out of the vehicle, look under the carpet to determine the condition of the floorpan and firewall. If moisture has gotten under the carpet, there's a good chance the sheet metal below is rusting. Areas of surface rust can be sanded or ground away and then treated with Naval Jelly or other similar rust treatment. Repair any areas that have rusted through by welding in a sheet metal patch. In either case, apply an epoxy primer and paint to help minimize the recurrence of rust. Floor panel patches for particular vehicles are available from a variety of sources; a competent sheet-metal worker can always make something up too.

Vehicles that have larger aftermarket support will have more panels to choose from, such as a portion of the floor

*Most seats are relatively easy to remove from the vehicle. Bucket seats usually have two bolts in the back and two in the front securing them to the floor. It may be necessary to slide the seat forward or backward to gain adequate access to these bolts.*

*When looking for salvage yard or swap meet seats, check to make sure the slider mechanisms are not damaged (at least not beyond repair) and that they work properly. Often, a little WD-40 or other spray-on lubricant works wonders to free sticking mechanisms.*

or a complete floorpan. Some vehicles, however, will be limited to a panel that is sufficient for repairing the typical amount of rust for that particular vehicle, which may be more or less than what you really need. Depending on the actual vehicle, you may be able to choose between a front floor, a rear floor, or a full floor that combines the two. You should buy a replacement panel larger than the hole that you are repairing just to make sure you are welding the

*Also check the alignment of the mounting brackets. These are designed to fit on a flat floor. Depending on the donor vehicle, some seats have mounting brackets that are longer on one side or the other. Or, it may be that your vehicle needs to have longer brackets on one side or the other. Neither situation is beyond adaptability, but if one set of seats will bolt right in while others require modification, make your life easier in choosing.*

replacement panel to solid material. There's no need to purchase and replace the entire floorboard if the damage is limited to one small hole. Look at the rust area carefully to determine the true extent of the damage. What may appear to be one small hole may prove to be a completely rusted floor upon closer inspection.

Installing patch panels is somewhat out of the realm of this book, but the basic procedure is first to determine the area that needs to be patched. Obtain a patch that is 2 to 6 inches larger than that area on all sides. Using a die grinder with a cutoff wheel, a sheet metal nibbler, a reciprocating saw, or a plasma cutter, and cut out the bad material, leaving enough material so that there is some overlap between the old and new. Then weld in the replacement panel by making small welds 6 to 8 inches apart, then welding in between the first welds. Different situations require different types of welds; refer to a good bodywork reference if you're not sure which approach is best. Always use caution not to weld in the presence of gasoline vapors, combustible upholstery material, or any other flammable substance.

## SEAT FRAMES AND SPRINGS

Whether you have taken the covering off of an old seat or are working with a new, aftermarket seat frame and springs,

now is the time to make sure that it is clean and in good condition. An aftermarket seat frame will probably just need to be wiped off if it has been sitting in your garage for a while. An older seat frame may need some substantial work before it is ready to be upholstered, however. You will need to remove any bird's nests, rat's nests, animal droppings, or any other animal remains. This may seem silly, but any automotive upholsterer can probably vouch for at least one occurrence of at least one of those situations.

Remove any unnecessary hog rings, staples, or other wires that may puncture upholstery material. If any springs are loose, they should be resecured to the framework. Does the sliding mechanism work smoothly? Damaged or bent tracks will need to be straightened or repaired. Does the seat back fold smoothly (if it is supposed to fold at all)? Some cleaning of dust and dirt along with a bit of lubrication (use silicone or other material that will not stain or otherwise damage new upholstery) will usually get the seat frame to work properly. Are the seat frame or springs excessively rusty? Surface rust can usually be removed by lightly sanding the metal, while heavy rust may require media blasting or a treatment of Naval Jelly or other rust dissolver. To keep rust from recurring, apply a coat or two of primer with a rust inhibitor, followed by a couple of coats of gloss black paint to make the seat frame look like new.

## ADDING PADDING

Stock replacement seat foam is available for some vehicles, yet a skilled upholsterer—or you—can make whatever is needed too. (Foam types are discussed in Chapter 3.) If you are replacing only small sections of foam—say on a torn seat rather than a worn-out one—you can shape foam of similar density into the correct contour and then glue it in place with contact cement. If you choose to be creative, you can add multiple layers of open-cell foam to shape the seat cushions and seat back to your specific design. Each layer of foam can be glued to the previous layer with contact cement.

Additional foam is typically placed into the lumbar region in the seat back. It may also be desirable to add a bolster around the edges of the cushion and back. Glue the foam together to reach the desired thickness and then cut it to the desired shape with a razor knife.

## MAKING PATTERNS

If the seat you are recovering is in fairly decent shape, you already have a pattern for the new seat cover. You will have to commit yourself to sacrificing your existing cover, however. Using a seam ripper or a pair of scissors, carefully rip the seams out of your existing cover to the point that it is a collection of individual pieces. Now that these pieces of

Here we see a seat being custom made to fit in this 1932 Ford roadster. The seat base and seat back are made of plywood (3/4 inch thick or thicker). Padding is open-cell foam that has been cut to shape to form a bolster at the front of the seat. This foam is fairly dense, so to add some cushioning effect, the seat cushion has a hole drilled in it at each intersecting grid point. This allows the foam to "give" a little bit, yet still be firm.

seat cover are in a two-dimensional shape rather than three-dimensional, they can be used for patterns.

If your existing seat cover is stretched excessively or is damaged too much to use as a pattern, you will need to make a new pattern. A new pattern can be made from Kraft paper, poster board, or scrap upholstery material.

When making patterns, it pays to think ahead if you are even considering doing upholstery work to anything other than the vehicle you are currently working on. If you think that you may be doing a similar-style vehicle with similar seats or door panels in the future, take the time to use a more durable material for the pattern. The savings in time of not having to make the same pattern a second time will make up for the extra time and perhaps money spent to make the pattern out of poster board, rather than quickly cutting one out of paper for a single use.

Begin by dismantling the seat assembly so that you have the seat cushion and the seat back separated. To assist in making your pattern symmetrical, use a piece of chalk to draw a centerline on the seat cushion and the seat back that you are recovering. Obviously, you will need to take some measurements to be sure this line is properly centered from side to side. On whatever you are using for a pattern, mark this same centerline.

Prior to making a pattern, determine how you actually plan to cover the seat, how many pieces will be involved, and how they will be sewn together. Some seat cushions, whether a bench or a bucket, have one piece of material that you sit on and a second panel that runs forward from one side, wraps around the front, and runs back on the other side. With a seam at the top edge of the seat on three sides, this style of seat cushion is easy for making a pattern. Another seat cover style involves a panel that continues to the front of the seat. This style requires that the side panels be stitched to the top and to the front. Being able to visualize the finished product will make pattern making easier.

Since several pieces of material will be sewn together and will be changing directions, it is critical that you make several reference marks while you are making your patterns. Some trimmers cut small notches in the material, while others use chalk marks (often accompanied by numbers). Whatever works for you is what matters, but you will need to have some way to verify that everything lines up correctly. When sewing, most trimmers line up the centerlines of the material and sew to the end. Then they return to the centerline and sew in the opposite direction to the other end. If you begin at one end and just start sewing, your alignment will most likely fall off center.

Now measure across the back of the seat cushion. On the pattern, mark a line perpendicular to the centerline and transfer the dimension of the back of the seat onto this line, keeping half of the dimension on each side of the centerline. Now measure the front to back dimension on the seat and transfer it to the centerline. From the centerline on the seat cushion, measure to the front corner of the seat. Now transfer this dimension to each side of the centerline from the front center of the pattern. Measure from the back corner of the seat cushion to the front corner, and then transfer this measurement to the pattern on each side. Now connect the dots with a pencil or marker. If you have followed the procedure correctly, the pattern will be the same size and shape as the top of the seat cushion. Before cutting out the pattern, add 1 to 2 inches outside of the cushion area around the entire pattern. This provides the necessary material for stitching. If the sides and front of the seat are the same height, measure the overall length and make a rectangular pattern that is the same size. Be sure to add 1 or 2 inches on all sides before cutting.

Make a pattern for the seat back using the same basic procedure. The big difference between the patterns for the seat back when compared to the seat cushion is that the seat back needs a front and back in most cases. The seat cushion needs a top, but doesn't require a bottom.

To better imagine the final look of the pattern described above, envision placing a flat-bottomed paper grocery bag over the seat back and another over the seat cushion. At each crease in the bag, there would be a seam, unless you choose to make the sides and top of the seat back or sides and front of the seat cushion from one single piece each.

There are several different types of seats and several ways to upholster each of them, so describing how to make a pattern for all of them would be a book in itself. Just remember to disassemble the seat cushion and seat back if they are indeed two separate pieces (some bucket seats are actually just one piece). If a bench seat has a split back, make a pattern for each side, whether they are removed from the seat or not. Remember to measure twice and cut once, as several bench seats are now split 60/40 rather than 50/50. Make patterns for folding armrests and headrests in similar fashion.

With all of your patterns made and cut out to the correct size (with an inch or two extra on all sides), place the patterns so that they do not overlap, but so that they make best use of the material you are working with. In other words, use material from one or two edges rather than cutting from the middle of a piece of material. Trace around each pattern piece with chalk or China marker onto the material. Pieces that are the same can use the same pattern, just be sure that you cut out enough pieces and that they are orientated properly. It will usually be necessary to flip the pattern for the opposite side. (This process is detailed with photographs in the accompanying sidebar.)

### CUTTING MATERIAL

When you have traced around all the patterns, use a sharp pair of scissors (or shears) and cut out each piece of material. Each piece of material also needs to have its own piece of scrim-backed foam, so unroll scrim-backed foam material of the appropriate thickness out onto the worktable. Just like when you were placing the patterns onto the upholstery material, place the material onto the foam. Leave some space between each piece. Cut out the foam material so that it is slightly oversize when compared to the upholstery material.

Fold over approximately half of the upholstery material, then spray the back of it and the front side of the foam with contact cement. Then press the two materials firmly together and press out any wrinkles with your hands. Now fold over the other half of the material and repeat the process. When each piece of material has been glued to a piece of foam, sew around the perimeter of each piece of material. Use a pair of scissors and cut off the excess foam. You are now ready to start sewing the pieces together to form your seat cover.

### MAKING THE SEAT COVER(S)

Prior to sewing, verify the order in which you will sew the pieces together. You want to be able to close off each seam in an attractive manner, while leaving enough of the cover open so that you can fit it over the seat frame. With the vast array of seats, there is no one method suitable for every seat. This is where a seasoned professional's experience makes a difference in the finished product.

If you plan to incorporate any sort of pattern or design, such as vertical or horizontal pleats, diamonds, squares, or a free-flowing form into the seat surface you must sew these elements into the cover before sewing the pieces together. (Determine what pattern you want before cutting the material and allow for any extra fabric the design requires at that time.) With the desired pleats sewn into the upholstery material, the various pieces can be aligned (remember the notches or alignment marks?) and sewn together. To hide the excess material at the seams, sew the cover from the inside, turning it right-side-out before you install it.

### INSTALLING THE COVER

The seat cover is now ready to be slipped over the seat cushion or seat back. Some upholsterers use talcum powder while others use material they call "slickum" to ease installation. The purpose of these additives is to allow the cover to slide over the foam more easily.

After the seat cover is slid onto the cushion, make sure that it is properly aligned and that all wrinkles are pressed out. The seat cover can now be secured to the seat. The usual way to do this is to make a "listing." A listing is a narrow strip of material folded over on itself lengthwise and sewn to the edge of the seat cover. Insert a metal rod or wire through the listing; this will provide a means of securing the cover to the seat frame with hog rings. The wire through the listing distributes the force exerted by the hog rings all along the fabric's edge so they don't tear through. Some newer seats have plastic clips that must be sewn to the lower edges of the cover and then they are hooked over the seat frame.

## REINSTALLING THE SEAT

To reinstall your freshly upholstered seat in your vehicle, enlist the help of another person. You may not need the help for a bucket seat, but a bench seat can be cumbersome to move and position by yourself.

If there is no carpet, floor mat, or other floor covering in place, it will be easy to see the bolt holes in the floor. More than likely, however, floor covering will at least somewhat obscure your vision of the bolt holes. Use an awl or ice pick to poke around to find the bolt holes. After finding one hole, set the seat into position with the appropriate mounting holes aligned. Rotate the seat slightly in each direction to find the bolt hole for the opposite corner mounting hole. With nonadjacent mounting holes aligned, the other two holes will align.

At each mounting hole location, use a razor knife to cut a small "X" in the carpet. Push the mounting bolt through the seat's mounting surface and thread it into the threaded insert or welded nut. On some custom vehicles, the seats actually may be secured with bolts that thread into nuts that are not welded to the underside of the floorpan. This approach requires that someone hold a wrench on this nut from underneath the vehicle to secure the seat.

### Seat risers

If you are using seats that are not original to your vehicle, the seats may not sit at the optimal angle to meet your needs. There are a couple of ways to deal with this. Adjustable seat risers are available that allow you to easily (although manually) adjust the tilt angle of your seat. Each seat requires two risers and each riser consists of two separate pieces of metal. Each of these are an "L" shape with mounting holes in the flange and adjustment slots in the web.

Bolts through the mounting holes secure the lower portion of the riser to the floor, while bolts through the upper mounting holes attach the seat. Bolts through the adjustment slots are loosened to adjust the tilt, and then tightened to hold the seat in the desired position. This method can also be used simply to raise the seat.

A second style of seat riser requires that you first determine the desired tilt angle (if any) in relation to the floor and the amount of rise that is desired in the seat. You can determine the best location for the seat by placing pieces of wooden 2x4s (or whatever you have lying around the shop) underneath the seat's mounting points. Add or remove spacers until the seat is at its most desirable location. Measure the total height of spacers at the front and back mounting locations. This determines the angle of the seat. Measure the distance between the front and rear mounting points of the seats, and the distance between the mounting holes in the floorpan.

With these horizontal and vertical dimensions sketched out, transfer them to a piece of ½-inch or wider flat aluminum stock. When the bracket is finished, it will be placed on its edge and should be in an exaggerated "I-beam" shape when viewed from the side. It should be obvious that the shape of the aluminum plate will vary depending upon the dimensions. Shape this new mounting bracket so that two holes can be drilled in the bottom flange to accept bolts to secure the riser to the floor. Shape the upper portion of the riser in similar fashion so that bolts can be installed through holes in the bracket and into the seat. Cut out the bracket with a plasma cutter or band saw, smooth the edges, and repeat the process so that you have two riser brackets for each seat. The aluminum bracket can be scuffed with a Scotch-Brite pad for a dull finish, polished for a shiny appearance, or anodized or painted to add some color. (The last photo in this chapter's sidebar, Reupholstering Traditional Bucket Seats, shows such a homemade bracket.)

## SEATBELTS

Although perhaps not as glamorous as a leather-covered bucket seat or finely crafted console, seatbelts are an important part of any automobile's interior. Federal law requires manufacturers to install them in new vehicles and many states require motorists to wear them. They are also important to many child-restraint systems. Installing them is simple and replacements are available for most popular cars.

Three-point shoulder harnesses are available from a number of suppliers at less than $100 per person with simple lap belts also available at even less expense. If your vehicle does not have seatbelts, you cannot blame difficulty of installation. For lap belts, drill two holes in the floorpan, while a three-point shoulder harness requires a third hole to be drilled in the B-pillar just behind the seat. To keep the bolts from pulling through the floor (or door pillar), an anchor plate should be used to spread potential stress over a larger area.

# REUPHOLSTERING A ONE-PIECE BUCKET SEAT

Professional upholsterer Don Albers covered a one-piece bucket seat for a reproduction Cobra. These seats don't have a typical seat frame or springs like most seats. They are a fiberglass shell covered in black vinyl. When the seats are finished, they bolt directly to a sliding mechanism that offers front to back adjustment only. Although not the most common seat to be recovering, the procedure shows a variety of techniques. (The following section shows the procedure for traditional bucket seats.)

Don begins by applying foam padding to the seat back, seat cushion area, and around the edges of the seat. He sprays contact cement onto the back side of the foam that will be secured to the edge of the seat cushion. Contact cement also will be applied to the fiberglass shell.

After the contact cement becomes tacky on both pieces (the foam and the fiberglass shell), the foam is pressed into position on the edge of the seat. Although the foam will be covered and won't actually be seen, each piece needs to be consistent in size and location as similar pieces on opposite sides.

Don applies more contact cement to the lower outside of the seat bucket. Portions of the area to be glued may dry completely before Don is ready to position that portion of the foam. This is not a problem; he simply applies more contact cement.

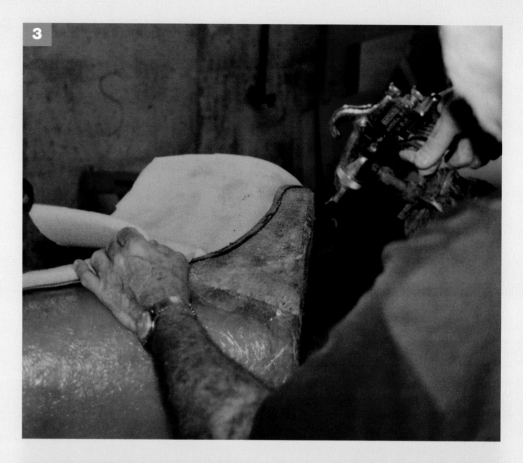

Don checks that location of the padding is consistent from side to side. A benefit of using contact cement is that if padding or material is not placed correctly, you can easily remove it, apply more contact cement, and reposition the piece.

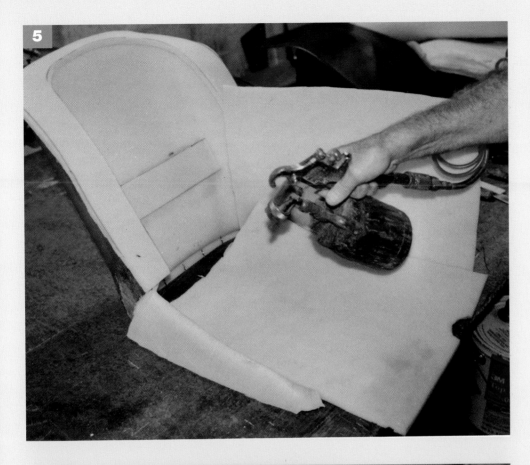

**5**

With the multiple contours of the fiberglass bucket, it is easier to build up the padding with thin layers, rather than attempt to wrap a thicker piece around the bucket. Don applies contact cement to the back of the foam with a cheap spray gun. No need for an expensive high-quality gun for this.

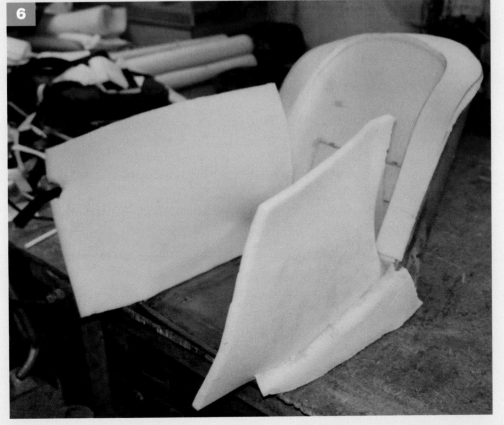

**6**

The common error most inexperienced trimmers make is that they don't allow the contact cement to become tacky before pressing the surfaces of both pieces together. This second layer of padding is allowed to dry a bit (not completely, but enough to become tacky) before Don presses it into place.

When the glue becomes tacky, the foam is pressed into place. Don applies the second layer of foam padding to the right side bolster of the seat.

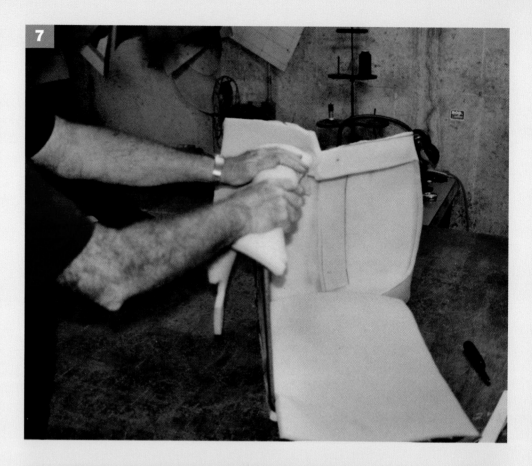

On the left side of the seat, the second layer of foam padding has yet to be wrapped down around the side to form the bolster and around the side to the back.

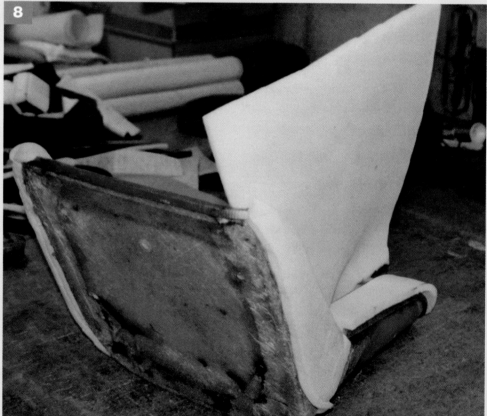

**9**

After applying contact cement to both the back side of the foam and the outer side of the seat shell, Don wraps the foam over the edge and presses it into place. He smoothes out any bubbles or wrinkles before the adhesive completely sets up.

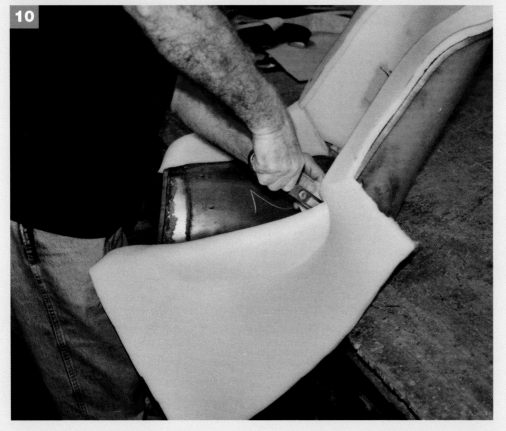

**10**

Don cuts off the excess foam from the inside of the seat area. This can be done with scissors (shears) or a razor knife.

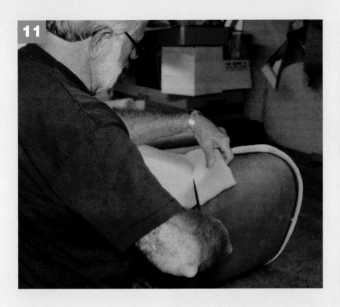

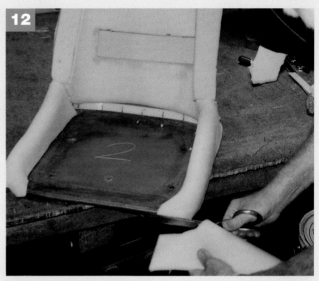

Don cuts off the excess foam that has overlapped onto the back side of the seat bucket. This particular piece of foam covers the side of the seat shell inside and out, but not the back.

It is necessary to trim excess foam from the front of the seat as well. Anywhere there is a layer of foam, there will be a distinct difference in the feel of the seat when compared to portions of the seat where there is no padding. An upholsterer must avoid errant overlaps of foam.

The seat bucket has all its padding attached and is ready to be covered. Each side bolster will be covered, and then a separate, removable cushion will be set in place for the actual seating surface. The seat back (both front and back) will be covered with one piece (actually a few pieces sewn together).

Don sews together the two pieces that will ultimately cover one of the side bolsters. One piece will cover the inside while the other covers the outside, with the seam between the two positioned along the top edge of the foam that is wrapped over the bolster.

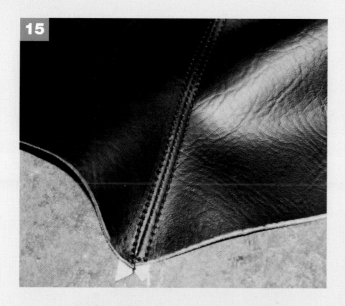

For strength when joining two pieces of material together, Don uses a French seam. You must allow for this type of seam when making your pattern and cutting out the material so that you have enough to sew the two pieces together properly.

To sew a French seam, place both pieces of material face to face and align the edges of the two pieces of material that are to be attached. Stitch the length of both pieces approximately 1/2 inch in from the edge. This stitch is what holds the two pieces of material together. To make this a stronger seam, turn the material right side up and stitch along both sides of this initial stitch, making sure that the top surface layer is sewn to the overlap created in the initial step.

One last look at the seat shell before it is covered with material. The fiberglass seat shell is approximately 1/2 inch thick, so you can see from this photo that the seat back is heavily padded. The horizontal strip across the back is an additional piece of high-density foam to provide additional lumbar support.

The cover for the left side bolster is now slid into position. It is too large, but can easily be trimmed to the correct size later. The side of the seat curves one way at the front and the opposite way at the back, so for now, it is important to fit the cover into the correct position.

With the bolster cover in place, the necessary trimming can begin. Do not get ahead of yourself when trimming off excess material. It is much easier to make another cut than it is to sew another cover together. For now, Don cuts off just enough so that the bolster cover can be positioned properly.

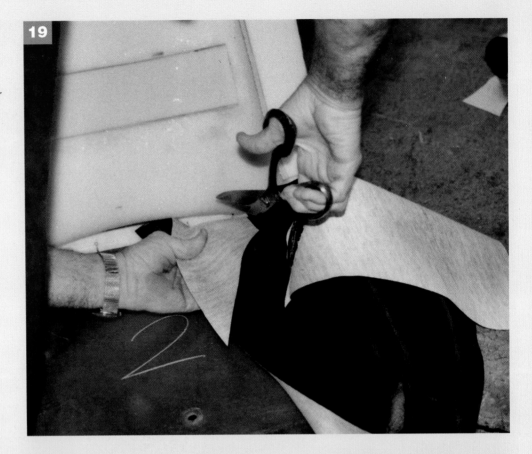

The back side of the inside bolster cover and the seat are sprayed with contact cement.

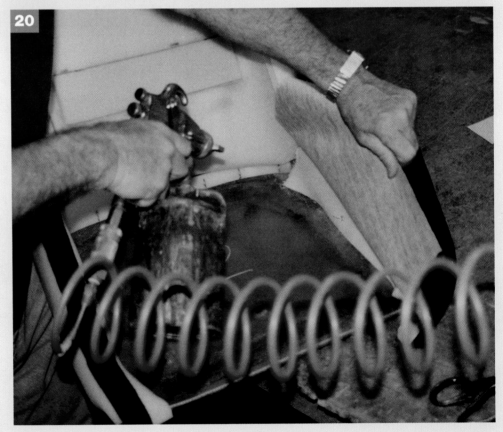

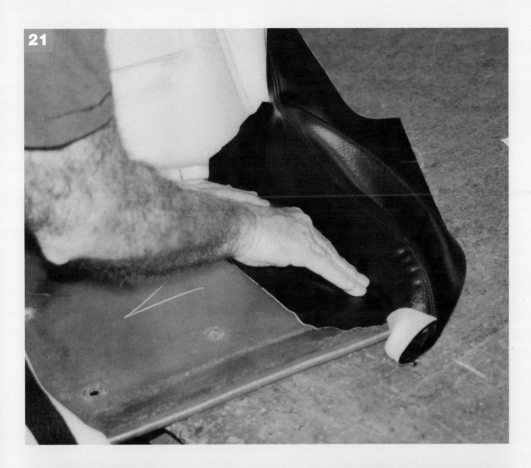

**21**

When the adhesive has dried to the point of being tacky, the bolster cover is pressed into place. The separate seat cushion will cover the excess material toward the middle of the seat.

**22**

Contact cement is now applied to the outside and bottom of the seat, as well as to the back side of the material. Contact cement dries quickly, so apply it only to the immediate area where you are working.

The holes in the bottom of the seat are for the mounting bolts that will attach the seat to the slider mechanism. This is part of the reason for the removable seat cushion.

Don pulls the bolster cover over the side and to the bottom of the seat. The seat sits extremely close to the floor, so the bolster cover only needs to cover the side and just a bit of the bottom.

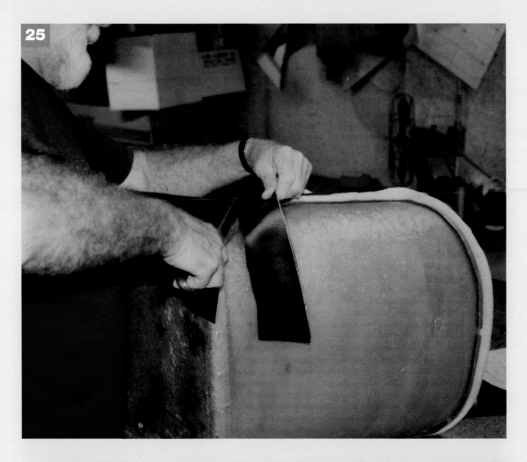

25

Since the seat back will be covered front and back with a cover, the excess from the bolster cover is trimmed away.

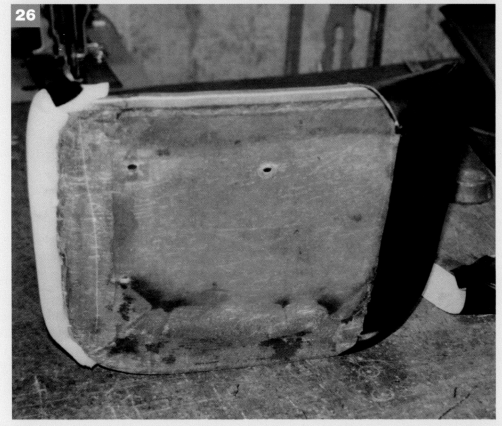

26

The bolster cover extends to just outside of the mounting bolt locations on the bottom of the seat.

After making a pattern and transferring it to the material, Don cuts out two pieces of material that will be the sides of the seat cushion cover. These, along with a pleated cover for the seat top, will make up the cover for the removable seat cushion.

The cover for the top and front of the seat cushion. An oversized piece of vinyl material has already been attached to a piece of open-cell foam. The pattern was marked on the material with chalk. The pleats are laid out and will be sewn past what will eventually be the edge of the material. The pleats on this seat are straight and parallel, but they don't have to be. The pleats could have been curved, although that might be more difficult to match on the other seat. Two chalk marks on the sides are alignment marks for the side pieces.

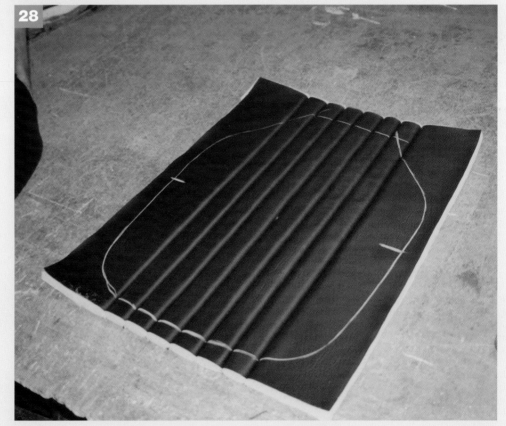

Don sews along the lines marked on the seat cover to create the pleats. Getting the pleats straight and evenly spaced is mandatory when doing professional upholstery.

Prior to cutting out the seat cushion top, Don sews around the perimeter, just inside of where the material will be cut. This is simply another step to ensure that the vinyl material stays attached to the foam beneath it.

With the vinyl material sewn to the foam padding, the seat cushion top is cut out. Take your time and be sure that you don't cut the stitches that outline the piece.

The completed seat cushion top before Don attaches the two side pieces. The narrow portion wraps down to cover the front of the seat cushion, while the side pieces attach to the angled portion and wrap around to the back and overlap in the middle.

**33**

To give the seat cushion a finished appearance where the top and sides connect, a bead (a.k.a. piping) is sewn first to the top piece, and then to the side piece. To make the piping, cut a piece of piping cord the necessary length and a piece of vinyl (in this case) the same length and about 1 inch wide. The necessary width depends on the actual size of the piping to be covered. The goal is to cover the bead and have from ¼ to a ½ inch of material overlap on each side. A stitch is then sewn along the piping, allowing you to sew adjacent pieces of material to the remaining flaps of material.

**34**

Using the alignment marks to match the side panel to the top cover, the two pieces are sewn together. To maintain the proper alignment, Don starts sewing at the alignment mark and stitches to one end. He then goes back to the alignment mark and stitches toward the opposite end.

Notice that while sewing, you are usually looking at the back side of the material. This is not a big deal, but something that you must be cognizant of when you plan the order of sewing pieces together.

With the first side panel sewn on and folded under, the second side panel is sewn on in the same manner. Align the pieces with the alignment marks and then sew from the middle toward both ends.

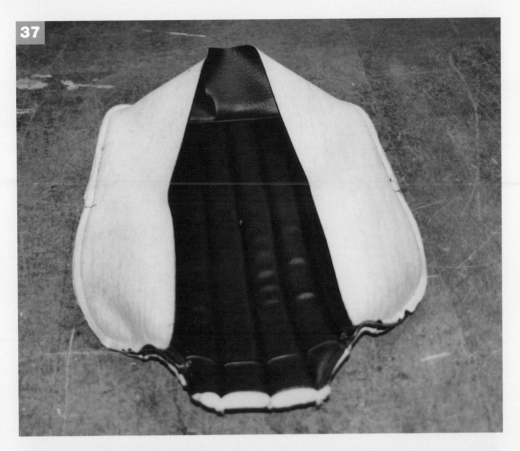

**37**

This is what the seat cushion cover looks like before being put on the seat cushion. The small tab will cover the front while the side panels will be turned down and attached to the bottom of the cushion.

**38**

Don uses a staple puller to remove old staples from the bottom of the seat cushion prior to covering it. Difficult to see in the photo, the staple puller looks much like a butter knife, but has several serrations in it to help grip staples to be removed.

The seat cushion cover is positioned on top of the seat cushion. The side panels are then pulled and pushed down over the sides and the back of the cushion to verify that the cover fits as it should.

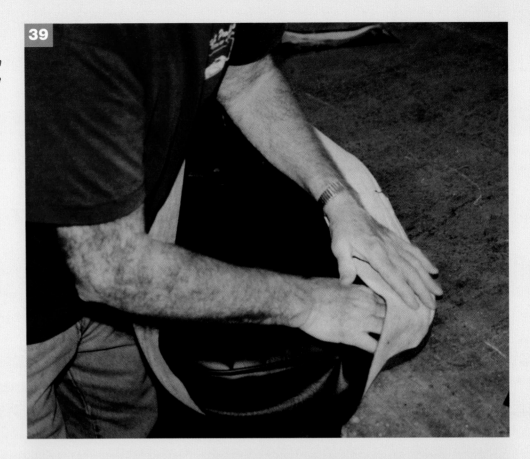

After verifying that the cover does indeed fit the cushion, the front of the cover is pulled back away from the cushion. Contact cement is applied to the cushion and the back side of the cover. Notice Don's use of a lead weight to hold the cover back while he applies contact cement.

**41**

With the adhesive applied, Don pulls the cover back into place, making sure that the piping aligns properly with the top edges of the cushion.

**42**

The seat top and front will be most visible, so this portion of the cover is pulled down around the front of the cushion and secured to the plywood base with staples. A pneumatic stapler makes quick work of this.

With the front secured, Don staples the side panels where they cover the back of the seat cushion.

Don begins working his way around the bottom of the cushion, placing staples approximately a staple width apart. Too many staples are not going to hurt anything. The staples are located approximately 3/4 of an inch in from the edge of the cushion.

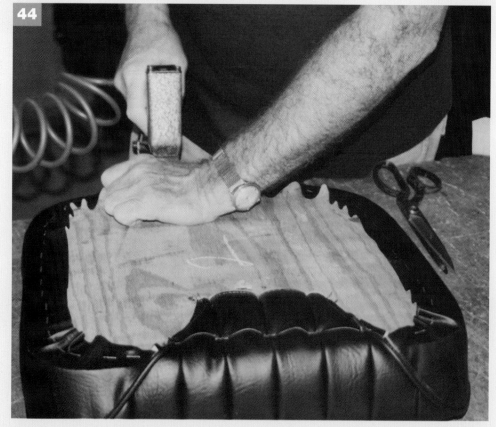

Use a razor knife to cut away the excess vinyl material on the underside of the seat cushion. Make this cut approximately 1/2 inch inside of the staples.

Don measures material to cover the right side seat bolster. This is the piece that will cover the fiberglass seat frame on the right side of the seat.

With the lines clearly marked with white China marker on the black vinyl, it is easy to cut out the strips of material.

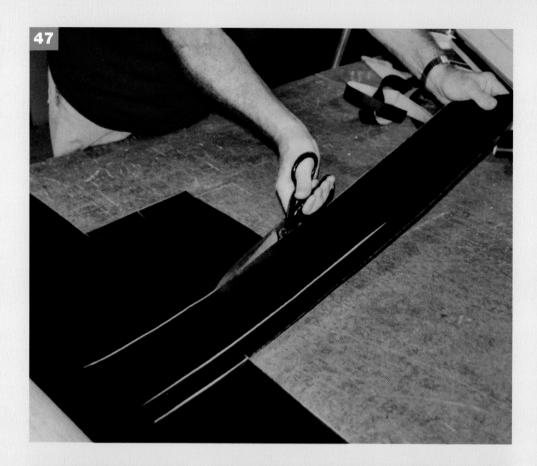

The vinyl material is attached to a piece of foam padding by applying contact cement to both pieces. One-half of the vinyl and one-half of the foam is sprayed, allowed to become tacky, then attached. Then the remaining half of the vinyl is attached in the same manner. After the vinyl is attached to the foam, the excess foam is trimmed off.

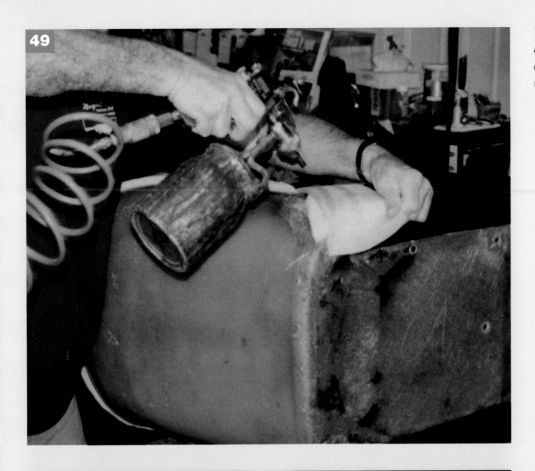

**49**

The foam-backed vinyl is now attached to both the inside and outside of the fiberglass seat with contact cement.

**50**

With the seat cushion made and the bottom of the seat frame covered, Don turns his attention to covering the seat back (both front and back). The basic procedure for covering the seat back will be sewing two large pieces that cover the front and back with a narrow strip of material between them that will allow for the thickness of the seat frame.

A pattern has already been made that is the same size and shape as the front of the seat back. The centerline is aligned with the centerline of the material and held in place with a couple of lead weights. Don traces around the pattern with a white China marker.

To help keep the vinyl material from separating from the foam, Don stitches around the perimeter of the piece prior to cutting it out. Care must be taken to ensure that the stitches are kept just inside of the cut.

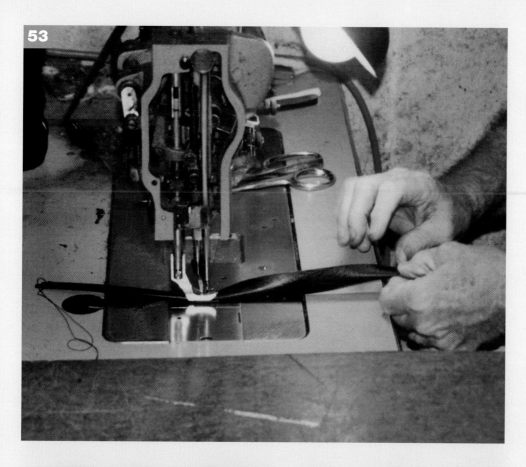

**53**

To help finish the seams on the seat back cover, piping will be sewn in. The piping is made by sewing a piece of oversized vinyl material around piping cord. The loose edges of material are what the adjacent pieces of material are sewn to.

**54**

After aligning the middle of the piping with the center of the front side of the seat back cover, Don sews the piping toward one side of the cover. When he reaches that end, he will return to the center and sew to the opposite end.

After sewing the piping to the front portion of the cover, Don sews the narrow strip of vinyl that will allow for the thickness of the seat frame to the remaining edge of the piping. To maintain alignment, Don begins in the center and sews toward each end.

Don continues sewing the "thickness strip" along the edge of the seat back cover.

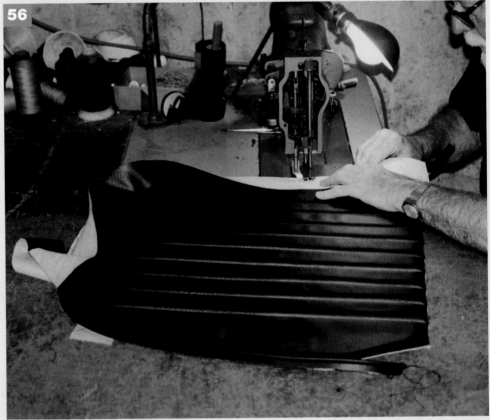

**57**

Just like on the pleated front cover, Don sews a strip of piping along the edge of the seat's smooth back cover.

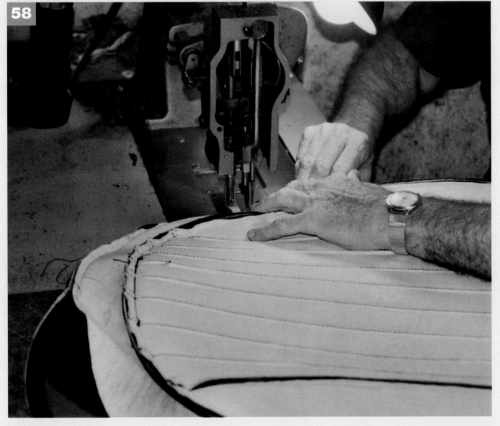

**58**

With the cover turned inside out, the front cover and narrow "thickness" strip are sewn to the piping on the back cover.

With all the seat back cover
pieces sewn together, the cover
must be turned right side out.

The back cover is pulled down
into place to check for proper fit.
Note how the sides are not sewn
together their entire length, but
left open at the bottom to flare
over the seat bolster. Another
reason for making reference
marks on patterns and the
material is so that going back
and ripping out stitches does not
become necessary.

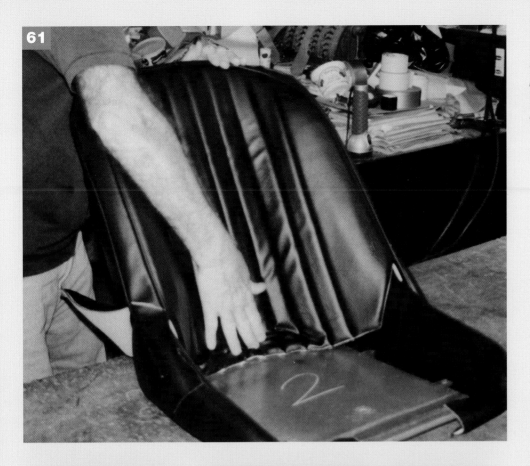

**61**

Take your time and make sure that the seat covers fit properly. Make sure that the seat cover is properly aligned on the seat and that the pleats run vertically, not askew.

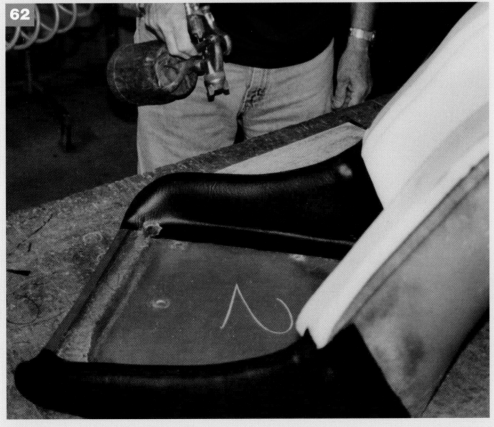

**62**

Don applies contact cement to one last piece of vinyl to cover the front edge of the bottom of the seat frame.

The vinyl material will be wrapped around the front edge of the fiberglass seat frame. The top of it will be covered when the seat cushion is in place, while the bottom edge of the material will be wrapped under the seat and out of sight.

The seat cushion is set into place to verify that the lower half of the seat frame is covered completely.

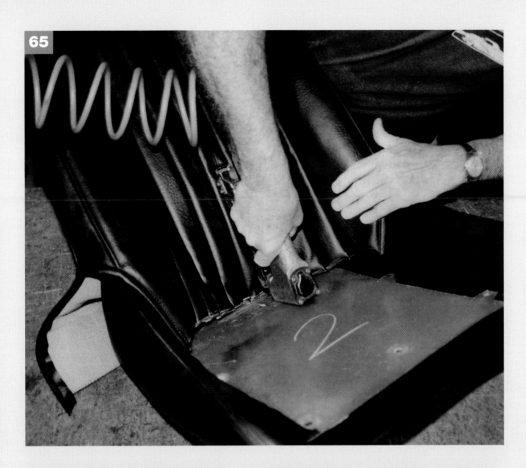

**65**

The seat cushion is removed, the seat back cover slid into position, and then stapled into place to prevent it from moving.

**66**

This is the seat without the seat cushion installed. Of course, after it is installed in the vehicle, the seat cushion most likely will not be removed—but for installation, the cushion being removable is a necessity.

A glimpse of the finished product. All that's left now is to install the seat in the vehicle.

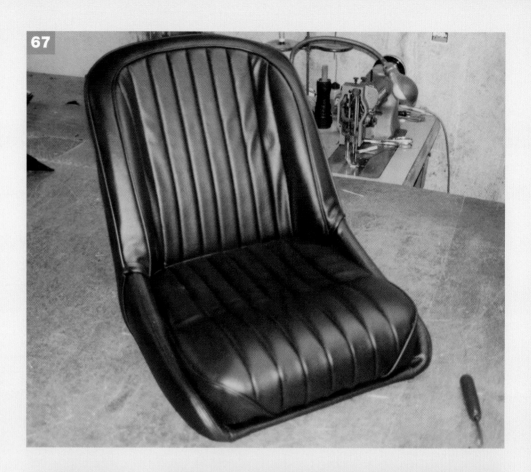

The seat is positioned in the vehicle. Bolt holes in the seat frame bottom align with mounting holes in the seat slider mechanism.

**69**

Minimal height between the floor and the bottom of the seat make this installation a test of wits, but most seat installations are fairly easy.

**70**

With the driver side seat bolted in, the choices are to go for a test drive or to finish covering the passenger seat.

# REUPHOLSTERING TRADITIONAL BUCKET SEATS

On this job, professional upholsterer Don Albers got help from apprentice Nick Mayden. Nick is a graduate of WyoTech (in Pennsylvania) and appears to have been paying attention in class. Nick and Don covered seats for a 1932 Ford Tudor street rod. Follow along as they demonstrate the ways to cover a pair of traditional bucket seats. A bench seat could be covered using the same basic procedure.

*After cutting out patterns for all the pieces required to cover the seat, the patterns are laid out on the material. To minimize waste, cut out all the patterns first, and then arrange them to make the best use of the material. You can get by with one pattern for pieces that are the same shape, but you must remember how the pattern needs to be oriented or you may end up with two left side flaps and none for the right side.*

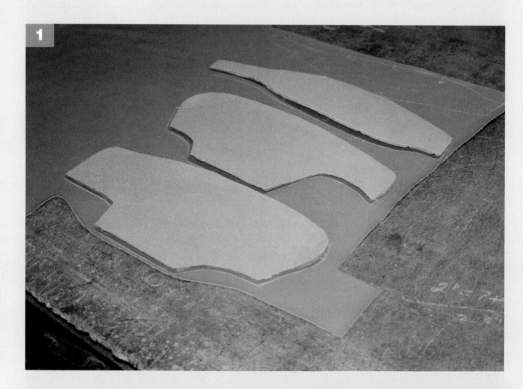

*Nick uses lead weights to help hold the pattern flush with the material while he traces around it with a white China marker. A China marker works best on vinyl or leather materials, while chalk works best on cloth or tweed materials.*

**3**

With all the pieces laid out and marked on the material, they can be cut out using a pair of upholstery shears. For now, cut the pieces slightly bigger than the pattern. Be careful not to cut into adjacent pieces.

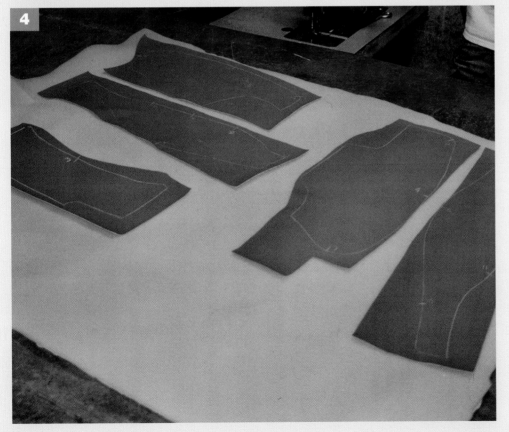

**4**

The oversized pieces of vinyl are laid out on open-cell foam that will pad the material. Always try to situate the pieces so that the minimal amount of material (foam in this case) is used.

Each piece of vinyl will need to be glued to the foam. Fold each piece of vinyl over on itself, then spray the back of the vinyl and the front of the foam with contact cement. After the glue becomes tacky, press the vinyl into place, smoothing out any wrinkles or bubbles. Then fold the opposite side of vinyl over, apply contact cement to the remaining vinyl and foam, and repeat.

With all the vinyl pieces glued to the foam, each piece may be cut out again. At this point, each piece should still be oversized.

**7**

To help keep the vinyl material and the foam attached, Nick stitches around the perimeter of each piece of vinyl.

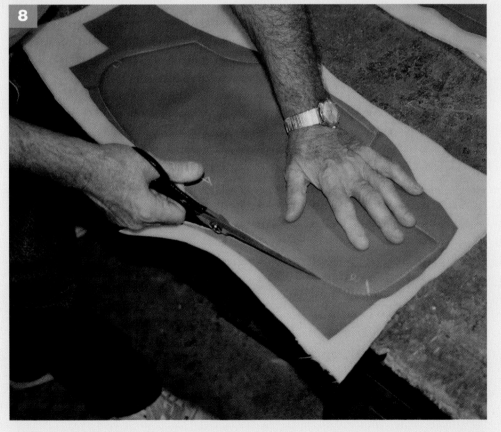

**8**

Once the perimeter of the material has been sewn to the foam, Nick cuts out each piece of vinyl to its actual size. Take your time and be sure that you don't cut inside of the stitching.

Take a close look at this piece of vinyl and you will see numbered reference marks. These will be used to properly align this piece with the pieces it attaches to.

The seats being recovered are molded foam and show some signs of wear. To smooth up the bolsters and to provide some additional cushion, a piece of open-cell foam is cut out to fit on the inside and outside of the seat's side bolsters.

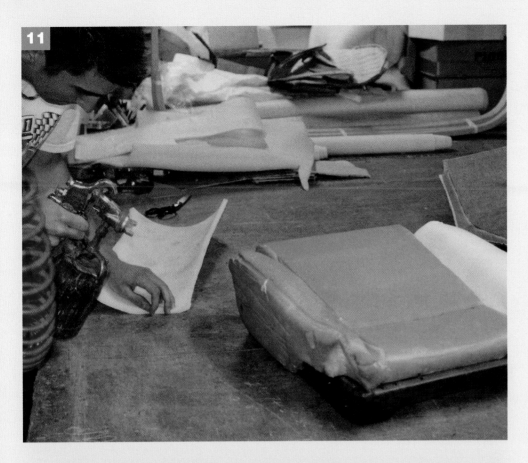

**11**

Contact cement is applied to both the outside of the molded-foam seat cushion and the back side of the foam that will cover it. Allow the adhesive to become tacky, then press it into position.

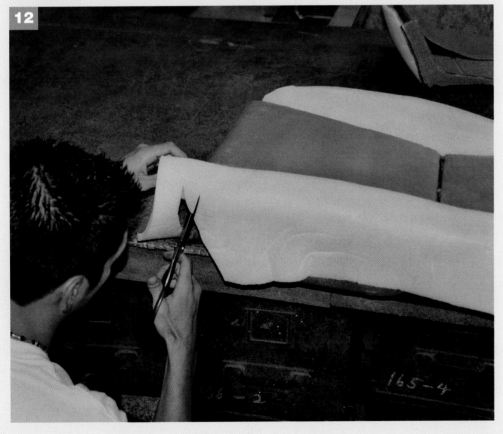

**12**

Nick carefully trims off any excess foam material using a pair of upholstery shears.

Remember those reference marks? On this side panel, the reference marks align with pleats in the front panel of the seat cover.

With both adjacent pieces positioned face to face, the edges of each piece of material are sewn together. To help ensure proper alignment, start at the middle reference point and sew toward one end. Then go back to the middle and sew toward the opposite end.

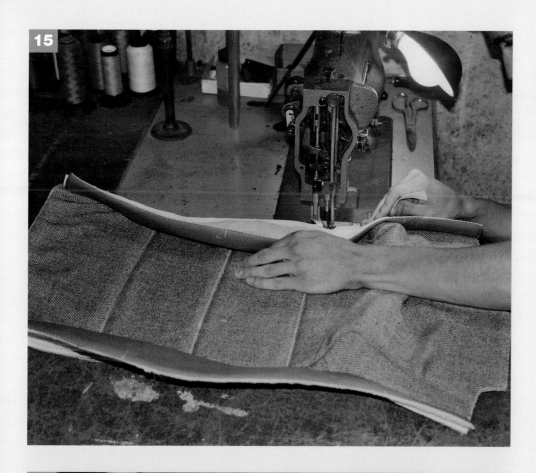

Sew on the opposite side panel using the same procedure. Align the reference marks, begin sewing in the middle, and work toward the ends.

Something all upholsterers should do, but many don't, is take the time to tie the threads at the end of a seam. Just an extra detail that doesn't take much time, but helps to keep seams from pulling loose.

The seat cushion cover is tried on for test fit. Verify that the cover is "square" with the cushion and is pulled down snug at all edges.

These particular seats originally had a piece of J-shaped hard plastic sewn onto the front edge of the seat cover that hooked onto the bottom of the molded-foam seat cushion to secure the cover in place. That piece has been removed from the original cover and is now sewn in place on the new covers.

**19**

The back of the seat cushion cover will be secured to the molded-foam seat cushion with hog rings. To give the hog rings something to attach to, a piece of listing is glued to the underside of the seat cushion cover. A thin steel wire will be slid through this listing. The hog rings will then wrap around this thin wire and another wire in the cushion, securing the seat cushion cover in the process.

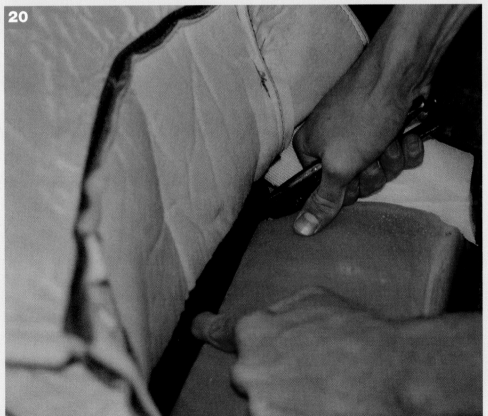

**20**

To help delineate the bolsters on the front and sides of the seat cushion, a piece of heavy-gauge wire stretches across the back of the front bolster and on the inside of the side bolsters, and is hooked onto the bottom of the seat frame. Another wire passes through listing material (black strip in this photo) on the seat cushion cover. This wire and the corresponding wire at the front bolster are hog ringed together.

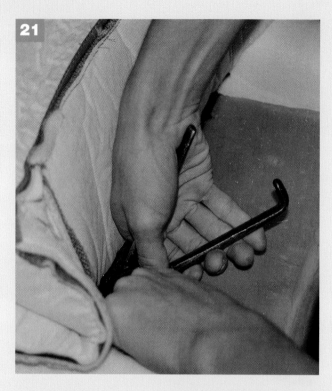

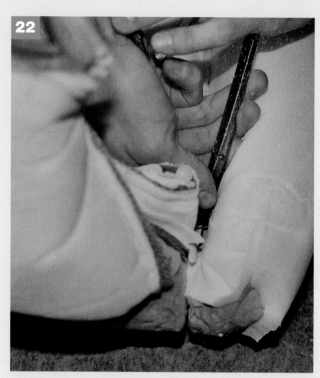

Nick uses a pair of hog ring pliers and hog rings to secure the seat cushion cover to the molded-foam seat cushion. It is necessary to make sure the hog ring goes around the wire in the listing for this to work.

Similar to the front bolster, the seat cushion cover is hog ringed to the wire that forms the side bolster. If not for these wires, the material would simply stretch across the foam, losing the shape of the bolster in the process.

Before hooking the cover to the seat cushion with hog rings, pull the material uniformly to the side of the seat.

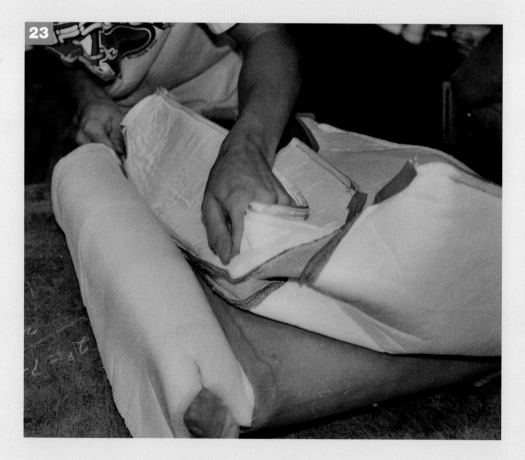

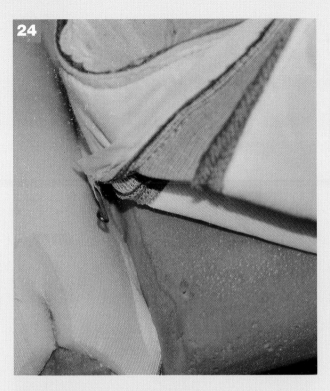

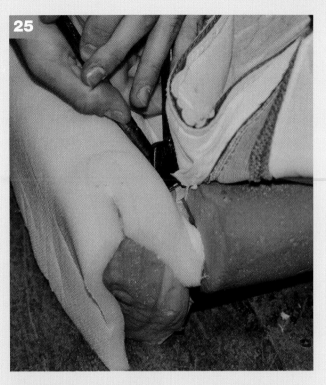

If you look closely near the middle of the photo, you can see the wire that will be hog ringed to the wire across the seat cushion.

The deeper the wire is pulled into the foam cushion of the seat, the more pronounced the bolster will be. This makes it more difficult to attach the hog rings, but is merely part of the job if a more pronounced bolster is desired.

With the bolster wires hog ringed together, the front and side flaps of the seat cushion cover can be folded over the edge of the seat.

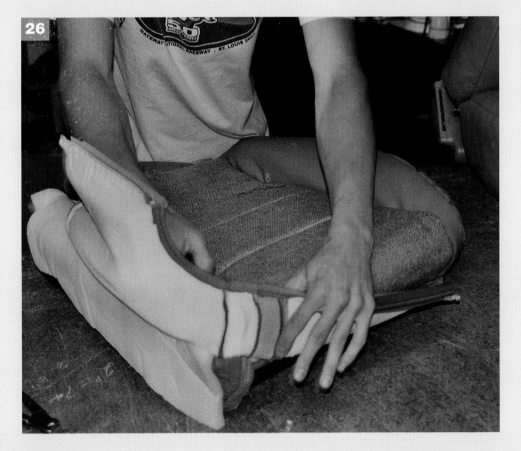

Nick checks the fit of the seat cover for any low spots in the seat cushion. Low spots need to be filled with foam padding material.

Nick feels that the very front of the seat is not full enough, so he cuts a piece of open-cell foam to the desired size.

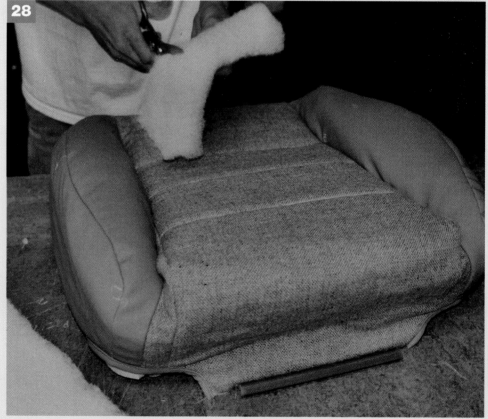

**29**

Prior to fastening the J-clips to the seat frame, any necessary extra foam is stuffed between the formed seat cushion and the seat cushion cover. Be sure to flatten the foam as necessary so that it blends into the area where it is needed, rather than looking like a wadded up ball of foam that sticks out.

**30**

The seat cushion is now secured in place by hooking the plastic J-clips over the edges of the metal seat frame beneath the seat. It doesn't matter if you start on the sides or the front and back, but work your way around the seat cushion by attaching opposite sides before attaching the remaining sides.

Double check the added foam to make sure that it has not moved out of its intended position prior to securing the seat cover over the cushion. It is better to go back and fix something now rather than later.

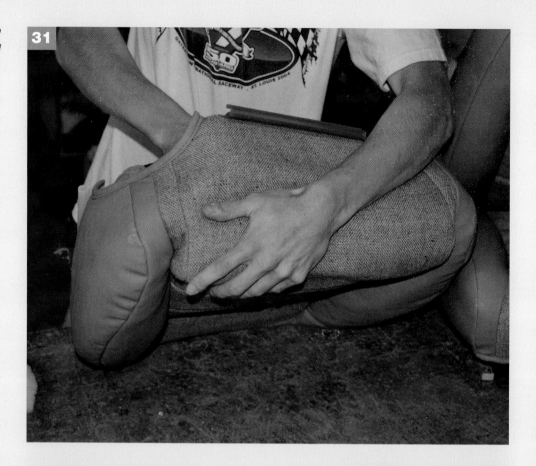

The front of the seat cushion looks much better now that the extra foam has been added and is properly positioned.

**33**

The sides are hooked into place by the J-clips. The two holes in the seat frame are for bolts that mount the hinge mechanism. They are left uncovered by upholstery material to prevent binding.

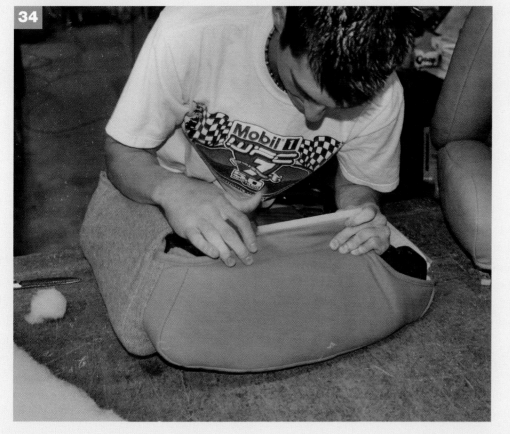

**34**

If you have made the seat cover correctly and have added the necessary foam to fill in any low spots in the molded seat cushion, the last side of the seat cushion cover should be a little snug to pull into position with the J-clips. Not that the cover should be extremely tight, but suitably snug.

With the seat cushion and seat back covered, the two portions of the seat need to be reassembled. Since you have taken the seats apart, you should know how to reassemble them. When disassembling seats, it may be a good idea to take some photos to refer to when it is time to reassemble them.

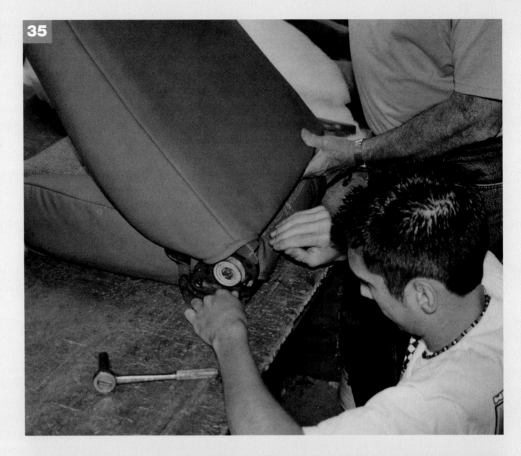

With these particular seats, reassembly basically consists of bolting the hinge mechanism to both the seat cushion and the seat back. A ratchet and correct size socket make easy work of these bolts. Be sure to start all bolts by hand to verify that they are not cross threaded.

**37**

The hinge mechanism is usually covered by a formed piece of metal or plastic trim. The trim is usually held in place by a few small screws that are easily reinstalled with a screwdriver—although it may require a Phillips, Torx, or some other specialty screwdriver.

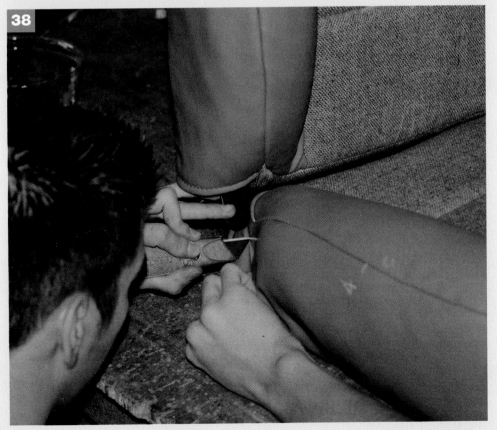

**38**

On the opposite side of the seat, one bolt is what secures the seat back to the seat cushion. To gain access to the hole for the bolt to be inserted into, Nick uses a razor knife to cut a small slit in the vinyl material that covers the seat cushion. Feel around for the hole before arbitrarily cutting a slit in the new upholstery.

With a small hole cut in the vinyl upholstery material, the bolt can be inserted into the bracket that attaches it to the seat cushion. Start the bolt by hand to make sure that no upholstery material is in the way and then tighten fully with a wrench.

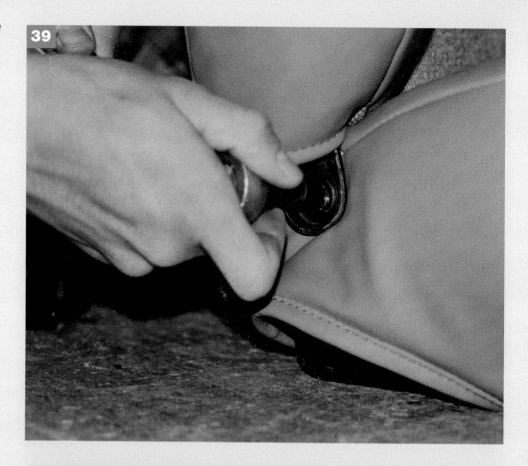

Just like on the first side, a piece of plastic or metal trim is used to cover the mounting brackets. Instead of using mounting screws, this cover plate is designed to snap in place over the heads of the bolts that are being covered.

**41**

This is the completed seat prior to being reinstalled in the vehicle. Although we don't show the procedure for making the seat back cover, it is made using the same procedure as that for the seat cushion.

**42**

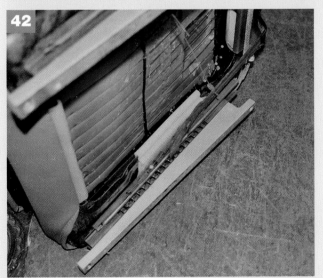

Although they would be simple to make, the seat risers/mounting brackets on these seats are the first of their kind that I remember seeing. They are cut out of aluminum and shaped to give the desired seat angle when bolted in place in the vehicle. Holes through the very front and very back allow them to be bolted to the vehicle's floor. Similar holes in the top half allow them to be bolted to the seat frame.

# INSTALLING SEATBELTS

Although they are federally mandated as standard equipment in all automobiles to be sold in the United States (since 1964), older vehicles may not have seatbelts, or you may choose to install new seatbelts for a variety of reasons. Older vehicles that have seatbelts may not have three-point shoulder harness belts that we are all accustomed to now. It may be that the vehicle is getting a different interior color scheme and you want the seatbelts to match the rest of the interior, or the seatbelts may have been damaged in an accident. Whatever the reason, installing new seatbelts is relatively easy, but there are some important things to know so that the newly installed seatbelts will do what they are supposed to do. Keith Moritz at Morfab Customs installed three-point shoulder harnesses in the two outer positions of the front seat in Vincent Sapp's 1964 Chevrolet station wagon.

*To determine a suitable mounting location for the outboard portion of the three-point shoulder harness, remove the interior panels from the upright panel (B-pillar) behind the door. Not seen in the photo is a mounting tab through which a bolt will be used to secure the retractor mechanism to the vehicle.*

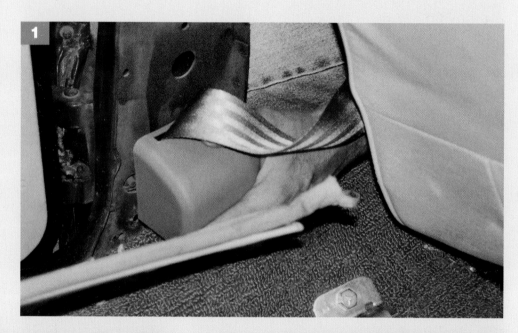

*To receive the bolt that will secure the retractor mechanism, a piece of flat plate that has a nut welded to the back side of it will be welded to the B-pillar near the floor. Here Keith has cut out the flat plate and drills a hole in the middle of it.*

*A seemingly minor point to some, but really an important step, is to smooth off all the sharp edges from the flat plate. Rounding the edges helps minimize the possibility of this plate tearing through the metal around it in the event of an accident.*

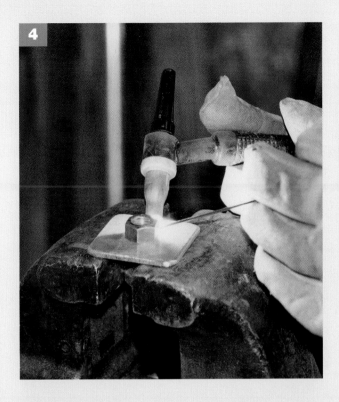

**4**

The thin plate is easy to weld to the vehicle's sheet metal, but is too thin to hold a seatbelt mounting bolt on its own. The strong solution is to weld a nut to the back side of the plate. Don't forget to chase the nut with a tap after welding to make sure that you don't break off any bolts in the nut.

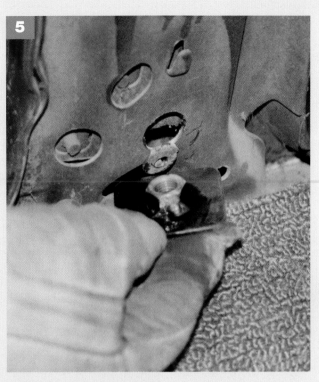

**5**

The flat plate with nut will fit nicely into this existing hole in the original sheet metal. The hole will allow the nut to fit inside of it, allowing the plate to be flush with the sheet metal.

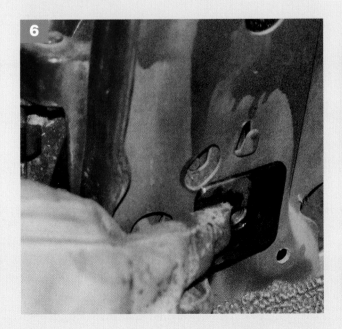

**6**

Keith checks the plate for proper fit with the sheet metal. Not necessary on this particular installation, but some installs may have necessitated some hammer manipulation of the plate to get the proper fit.

**7**

It takes two hands to TIG weld and this would be a difficult situation to fit a clamp, so a hammer was called into service to hold the plate in position while the initial weld is made.

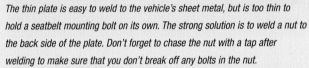

After a tack weld is made to secure the plate, the hammer can be removed, and the plate is completely welded into position.

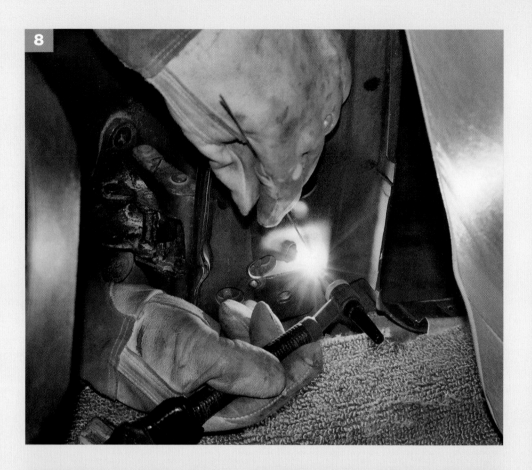

With the lower end of the seatbelt retractor squared away, Keith turns his attention to mounting the third point of the three-point shoulder harness. Unlike the bottom mounting point, there is no existing hole at the top. A hole is drilled to accept the bolt that will secure the upper portion of the belt.

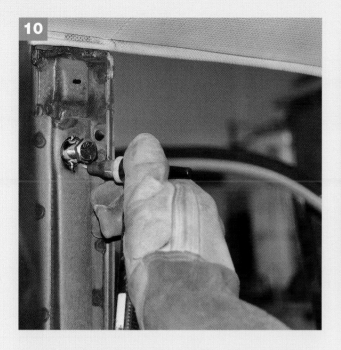

**10**

**11**

*Above left: This mounting point could be completed exactly like the lower one with a plate and nut welded in place. However, Keith chose to weld a nut inside the hole just drilled inside of the B-pillar, without the plate. The bolt is threaded into the nut to give Keith something to hold on to until the first tack weld is made. With the tack weld completed, the bolt is removed*

*and the nut is completely welded in place with some room between the nut and the vehicle's sheet metal behind it. After welding is completed, the nut is chased with a tap to clean the threads. Above right: The bolt is now reinstalled with the shoulder belt bracket installed.*

**12**

*The lower seatbelt retractor is now secured in place with one of the bolts included with the seatbelts, threaded into the newly constructed mounting point. The lap belt is bolted in place using the original mounting bolt location.*

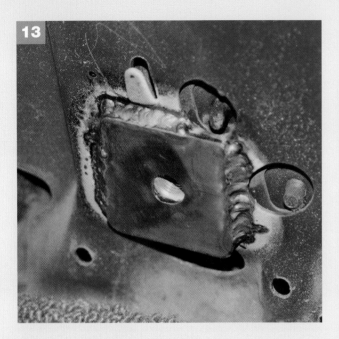

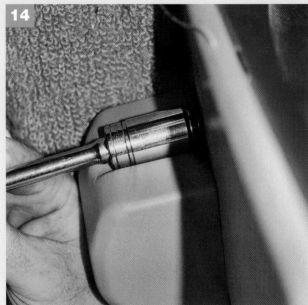

A close-up view of what the lower mounting plate looks like after being welded in place. The seat and shoulder belt must be removed to reinstall the upholstered panels.

After reinstalling the interior panel and securing it to the vehicle with the appropriate hardware, Keith secures the lower retractor in place. Note that in this photo, the retractor has been rotated approximately 90 degrees in order to reveal the bolt and the wrench used to tighten it. Before being completely tightened, the retractor will need to be rotated back to its vertical orientation.

Next, the upper bracket is reinstalled and secured with the supplied mounting bolt.

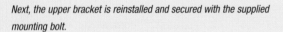

**16**

Both ends of the lap portion of the seatbelt are secured with bolts through the original seatbelt mounting holes in the floor. It may be necessary to poke through the carpet with an awl to find the holes, or actually locate the holes from below.

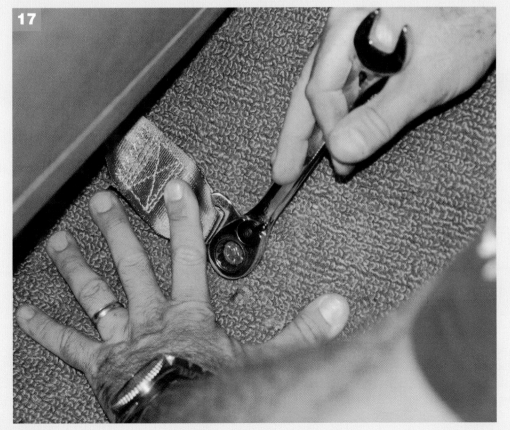

**17**

After finding the hole, remove any carpet or padding that would interfere with insertion of the bolt. Pass the bolt through the seatbelt mounting bracket, make sure that the bolt is not cross threaded, and tighten completely.

# CHAPTER 6
# DOOR PANELS

**D**oor panels came into being simply as a method of covering the window riser and door latch mechanism access holes. Upholstery on these cover panels ranges from nonexistent to extremely elaborate. A common example of nonexistent is the stock configuration on most early 1960s pickup trucks. Most of these trucks had a steel panel that could be removed to access door and window mechanisms. This panel was painted the same color as the rest of the interior, or a complementary color. A step up from this barebones approach was to upholster this removable panel. This can be done easily by attaching vinyl or tweed material.

As vehicles became more plush, door panels started covering more of the door's inside than just the access holes. These larger panels were initially flat and made of cardboard or thin plywood. They were typically covered with vinyl in some sort of pleated pattern. The next trend was formed plastic panels molded in the vehicle's interior color. As you moved up the trim levels on any particular model, these panels might include some upholstered inserts and sometimes some carpet on the lower portions. Contemporary door panels are a composite material that is molded into a neutral color or covered with the same material as the rest of the interior.

More elaborate door panels still cover those aforementioned access holes, yet do much more. A typical modern door panel serves as a mounting point for door handles, window riser handles, armrests, map pockets, stereo speakers, and cup holders.

## REMOVAL AND REINSTALLATION

Some door panels are held in place by screws that are easy to find and therefore easy to remove. Other panels are held in place by hidden clips that can prove to be humbling. If you cannot readily see screws securing the door panels in place, check out a vehicle-specific repair manual to determine how to remove these clips. Once you figure out where the clips are located and how they operate, they are not too bad to deal with. Avoid using excessive force to remove hidden clips because replacements may be difficult to find if you break the originals. Quite often, a specific clip removal tool is necessary. If this is the case, face the situation and buy the tool, as it will make your job much easier.

Old Chevrolets (and presumably others) from the mid-1930s up through the early 1960s used special serrated nail clips to hold door panels in place. These clips are difficult to remove without damaging them. The originals were

The door panel on this late-1950s Ford is typical of cars from that era. Both the seat and the door panel are covered with similar material (vinyl in this case) and have similar sized pleats. A tasteful design element is the combination of smooth and pleated areas divided with stainless-steel trim.

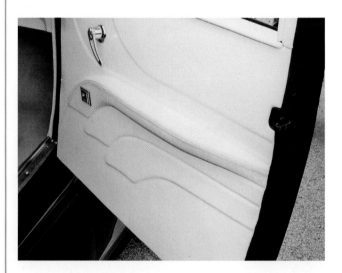

Many upholsterers consider this style of door panel a "hard" style. Not that it is difficult to do, but it's the opposite of soft and cushy. This door panel would be on the easier end of the difficulty scale. Multiple layers of closed-cell foam have been glued together and then covered to create this door panel. To align the multiple layers, use registration marks or alignment pins.

ical so that they align with small slits in the door's inner sheet metal.

## USING AFTERMARKET PANELS OR MAKING YOUR OWN

Aiming mainly at the street rod and classic truck market, Rod Doors manufactures ABS door panels for the do-it-yourselfer. These door panels are available with a variety of patterns molded into them. They could be painted for an extremely Spartan interior; however, they are designed to be covered with the material of your choice. The real beauty of these panels is that in addition to their three-dimensional shape, they can be covered with different material on different portions for a custom look. An example might be to have a band of carpet along the bottom of the door panel. The rest of the door panel might be covered with leather or vinyl in a matching color, with an insert of pleated leather or vinyl in a contrasting color.

For each upholstery material, you cut the portion to be covered from the main panel with a razor knife. Each portion may be cut to whatever shape you desire, as long as you can duplicate the design from one side to the other. Designs can either have straight edges or be free-flowing.

After determining the shape you want for each portion of the panel, cut out each shape. Depending on your method of cutting the ABS panel, lightly sand the edges to keep rough edges from cutting through the upholstery material. Cut the upholstery material slightly oversize, allowing 1 to 2 inches to overhang the panel all around its

*This door features some hard styling and some traditional pleats as an accent. Notice how the armrest is concentric with the upper line of the pleated insert and how the window riser and door handle are mounted to continue that arc. If the armrest/door pull was mounted in a horizontal position, this door panel would not look as good.*

strips of metal with "nails" attached. The strips went around the entire perimeter of the door panel. Replacements are available, but consist of short strips with a single nail in each strip. Placement of these on the panel is crit-

*Just how many components are incorporated into this late-model door panel? The armrest transitions into a door pull, while a stereo speaker serves as the front portion of a map pocket. Although this is an OEM door panel, it is produced in much the same way as aftermarket door panels found in street rods. Various sub-panels are covered with different fabrics or patterns and assembled to form the overall door panel.*

**DOOR PANELS**

Many door panels from the last three or four decades are made from a formed piece of plastic or vinyl molded in the desired color. Modern molding processes allow manufacturers to make three-dimensional door panels of virtually any design.

perimeter. Apply contact cement to the material and the bare panel. After the adhesive becomes tacky, apply the material to the panel and smooth out any wrinkles or bubbles with a small roller (a wallpaper roller works well). Fold the excess material over to the back of the panel and glue it there in the same manner. After all the "pieces" of the door panel "puzzle" are covered, they should be reassembled and held together with clips that are supplied with the panels. The reassembled panel is then secured to the inside of the door with heavy-duty hook and loop material.

On the back side of this late-model door panel we can get a better look at how it's constructed. It begins as a formed plastic panel with composite material used as structural support. At the lower right is the back side of a stereo speaker. The blue circles are mounting points where screws secure the panel to the door.

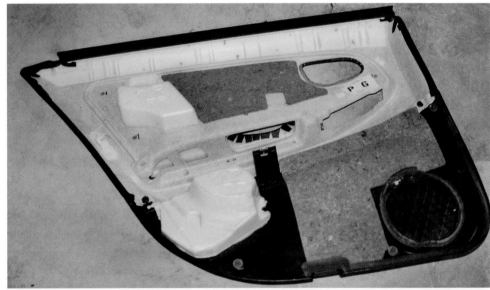

The back side of this early Camaro door panel shows why many of these need to be replaced. It is made from thin cardboard covered with cloth or vinyl held in place with clips. A little bit of moisture can do damage, while increased amounts of water inside the door can cause these panels to wrinkle severely.

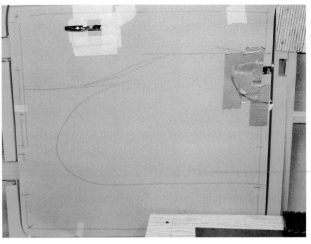

Above: It's difficult to see in the photo, but inside of this door pull is a screw to hold the door panel in place. Some attachment screws are in plain view while others are hidden. Remove the obvious screws first, and then if the panel still doesn't come off easily, look in the area where the door panel seems to be sticking to and find those screws that may be hiding.

The pattern for a custom door panel in Don Albers' shop. A piece of poster board has been cut out to the correct size and shape of the door. Marks around the edge of the door panel represent locations for screws to hold it in place when finished. Near the top of the door panel, cuts have been made so that the door release handle can protrude through the door panel. When all the necessary cuts have been made on the pattern, everything will be transferred to a piece of panel board for the actual door panel.

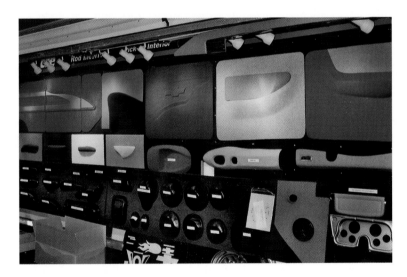

Upholstery supply companies often display their products at large automotive events, which provide enthusiasts a great opportunity to see what is available and to ask questions. This company is a dealer for Rod Doors and had a large selection of their products on display. The large panels across the top are door panels that can be covered in the materials of your choosing. Through the middle of the display are some covered armrests, an overhead console, and floor consoles. Across the bottom are uncovered armrests and speaker pods. The three-piece door panel at the upper left includes panels for the kick panel, the door, and a rear door or side panel with the design flowing around the back of the car. It was designed by the author for his 1929 Ford Model A sedan delivery as seen in How to Build a Hot Rod Model A Ford (MBI Publishing Company).

These Rod Doors panels make it easy for the do-it-yourselfer to finish off door panels with nice results. As with anything that is mass-produced, panels of any particular style (there are several to choose from) may tend to look alike, even though they have been customized by the upholsterer. This is in no way detrimental to the quality of the interior of your vehicle, but if you desire a truly unique interior, you may choose to build your very own, one-of-a-kind door panels. Fortunately, making your own door panels is fairly easy.

The first step in making a door panel is to cut a piece of plywood, Masonite, or panel board material to the appropriate shape and size. Whatever material you use, it should be approximately ⅛ inch thick. If the door panel is square such as on a Model A Ford, take a few measurements, then transfer them directly to the door panel. Where angles or curves come into play, make a pattern out of chipboard or poster board first. Do this either by cutting out a piece that is too large and trimming it down to the correct size and shape, or by taping pieces together until you get the

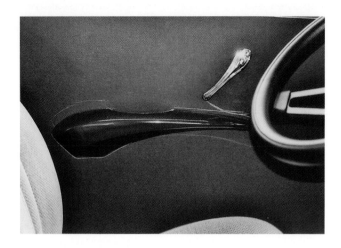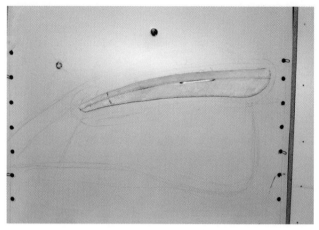

*Above left: This door panel under construction shows an important step. Above the armrest is a somewhat faded chalk outline of the original location for the armrest. Notice how the front edge of that outline would conflict with movement of the inside door release handle as indicated by the chalk arc. Instead of rotating the armrest downward in front, it was decided to lower the armrest enough to not be in conflict with the door handle. It is much better to find out this type of stuff early in the process than after all the upholstery is in place. Above right: With panel board held in place with push-in clips, the design for this door panel is roughed in. The shape and location of the armrest has already been determined, and the armrest attached to the panel. The dark spot near the top of the panel is the shaft for the inside door release handle, while the lighter colored spot is the shaft for the window riser handle.*

desired proportions. Pieces of scrap chipboard can be positioned around the periphery of the door and held in place with masking tape to establish the panel's outside edge. Cut the corners as necessary to achieve the correct fit, and then tape pieces in the middle to fill out the pattern.

When the pattern is completed, trace around it onto the material you will use for the door panel. Use appropriate tools and safety equipment when cutting out the panel. Now, do yourself a favor and test fit the panel to the door. Be sure to allow for the additional thickness of the padding and the material.

Whether you use prefabricated door panels or make your own, it is essential that they are the correct size. They cannot extend past the edges of the door at any location, as this will obviously make the doors difficult to open. Most any material used for door panels can be "shrunk" slightly by shaving off some of the edge(s) with an electric or pneumatic grinder or some sort of file, depending on the material. If you ignore the fact that the door panels are too large and force them to fit around the edges, the door panel will bow, placing stress on the fasteners. If you used plastic clips to secure the door panel, this constant stress will eventually break them.

Before covering the panel, determine how you will attach it to the door. For example, you may need to drill holes or secure clips to the panel's back side. Using the same approach as the factory did for the stock panel may be easiest, if your custom panel is the same thickness. Otherwise various aftermarket clips and other fasteners are avail-able. With the panel cut to fit and your attachment method established, you may begin the actual layout.

You may need to cut out the door panel to allow for door handle movement on newer style doors, or drill a hole for the handle shaft on older style door handles that fit over a shaft. With this latter style, mark the handle's range of movement on the panel before you plan its final layout to avoid interference. Do the same with the window cranks.

On older vehicles where the door handle simply slips over a round splined or square shaft, the handle can be set in place at most any orientation around the axis of the shaft. It is common for the handle to hang straight down while the door is latched, but nothing says that it has to be. This may be good to know if you begin running into interference issues with armrests. Extending the handle upward may provide the extra room to make the armrest work as an armrest.

Once you know where the door handles and window crank will go, you can determine where to place such things as armrests, door pulls, stereo speakers, and any other features you plan to incorporate. When placing armrests, give some thought as to how you sit in your vehicle. For example, I (along with lots of other drivers) rest my left elbow on the door window opening while driving my pickup truck. In my wife's vehicle, the seat is too low compared to the window opening for this to be comfortable, yet the armrest on the door is a little too low. These are minor annoyances in a stock vehicle. But if you're redesigning the interior space just for you, make things as comfortable as possible.

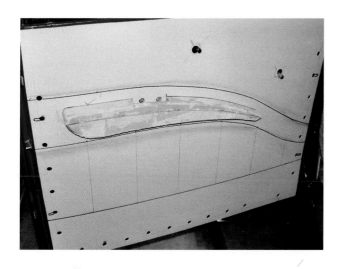 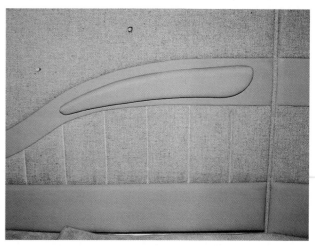

*Above left: On the other door, we get a look at the pattern that ultimately would be chosen. The armrest is still in the same location, but its shape will be continued throughout the door with a smooth layer of vinyl. Cloth will be applied above and below the vinyl, but will have vertical pleats on the lower portion of the door as indicated by the lines. The bottom 5 or 6 inches will be covered with vinyl. Above right: The finished door panel. Smooth vinyl around the armrest extends forward to the kick panel and rearward on the inside of the quarter panel.*

You also need to decide if the armrest will be covered separately from the door and then attached prior to final assembly, or if the armrest will become an integral portion of the door panel. Armrests are available in a variety of shapes, sizes, and materials, or of course, you can make your own from whatever material you are comfortable working with. Separate armrests can be drilled and tapped to accept a couple of bolts from the back of the door panel after it is covered, but prior to its being installed on the door.

Even though door pulls can be one of many different designs, they are an essential part of your door panel. Unless you are always going to have a chauffeur to close the door behind you, you will need some way to pull the door closed. Model A Fords had a small tab formed into the door window garnish molding; other vehicles use some sort of pull strap or handle, while some use the armrest as a door pull. Any of these methods works better than rolling down the window just to close the door. Make sure that the door pull is securely attached to the door and that attachment bolts are kept tight so that they don't strip out and allow the door pull to break off. Some thread-locking compound or lock washers—or both—will keep things secure for a long time.

Stereo speakers can be mounted in the doors, but you should follow certain precautions. Anytime you pass electrical wiring (including speaker wires) through sheet metal, use a rubber grommet to protect the wire's insulation from the hole's sharp edges. Without a grommet, the metal edge eventually will strip off the insulation and cause a short. Be sure to leave enough slack in the wires so the door can open all the way without pulling on them.

Since doors are prone to being slammed shut, take extra care to ensure that door-mounted speakers stay put. Use lock washers, lock nuts, thread-locking compound, or some combination to keep these fasteners snug.

Once you determine the location of all these extras in your door panels, you can decide what pattern (if any) you want to use in your upholstery. Do you want the panel to be covered, or do you want to add pleats to give it some depth? Do not be afraid to tape a piece of drawing paper over your door panel and sketch several designs on it before making your decision. Be sure to mark reference points on the door panel, pattern, and ultimately fabric covering the door panel so everything is aligned when you are finished. Make enough alignment marks so that the covering may be glued in place one-half at a time.

How you cover the door panels will depend on whether you have an upholstery-quality sewing machine. If you do, you can make the door panel in much the same way that you made the seat covers—that is, cut out the pieces of foam padding and the upholstery material, glue them together, and sew around the edge. If you take this approach, you can cover the door panel with a variety of fabrics and shapes, so long as the sum of the parts is equal to the overall size of the door panel plus 1 inch on all sides. If you want pleats in the door panels, you can lay them out on the fabric with a piece of chalk and then sew along these lines. When the overall door panel design has been

*Compare the drawing on the panel board with the finished door panel. By using two different materials in complementary shades and in differing shapes, a nicely done door panel has evolved. Missing only the inside door and window riser handles, it is a clean design that is cleaned up even more with hidden clips to attach it to the door. If the screws would be seen, consistent spacing would be critical to the door panel's overall appearance.*

*Part of the display at this interior supply vendor is a wide variety of molded plastic armrests. Most of them have a flange around their edge, allowing them to be glued or screwed to the door panel as necessary. Armrests are easy enough to make by cutting a piece of wood to the shape that you desire, but if you can find something that you like and it is already available, you can save time by purchasing a prefabricated piece.*

completed, whether one piece of material or several, it needs to be attached to the door panel itself.

Spray approximately half of the back of the door panel covering and the appropriate half of the door panel with contact cement and let it become tacky. Place the covering on the door panel and verify that all the alignment marks line up. Press out any wrinkles or bubbles with a roller, keeping the marks aligned. After this half of the door panel has been glued into place, spray contact cement onto the remaining half of the material and the door panel. When the glue becomes tacky, press the material into place, working out any wrinkles. At this point, you should have approximately 1 inch of material remaining all the way around the door panel. Any more than an inch should be cut off. Apply contact cement to the back side of the door panel and to the back of the remaining material. Wrap the material over the edge of the door panel and press it into place. It will be necessary to cut small slits into the material when you go around corners to prevent the material from puckering. Just be sure that the cut does not extend onto the front side.

If you do not have access to an upholstery-quality sewing machine, you can still cover the door panel with fabric. You just won't be able to have sewn pleats in it. However, you may choose to make it a multi-layered panel by adding different thicknesses or number of layers of high-density foam or lauan plywood to certain areas. When making a multi-layered panel, the key to a good job is to avoid intricate shapes, opting more for smooth, large-radius curves.

When you have cut your door panel to size, it is still a flat piece. To verify that contours of the additional foam or plywood are the same on both doors, make a pattern on a piece of Kraft paper, tag board, or poster board that is large enough to cover the entire door panel. The outer line will match the face of the door panel. Additional lines will indicate the edges of additional layers of material that will be glued to the layer below. As additional layers are added, transfer alignment marks from the pattern to the material and the door panel. This can be done easily with small holes and alignment pins. (Finishing nails work well to align the various panels.) Each piece of high-density foam or lauan plywood is then glued in place with contact cement. To avoid a stair-step appearance, the edges of the layers will need to be sanded smooth to blend into each other after the contact cement has dried. If you do want a pronounced step, round the edge of the top piece slightly. With the door panel now shaped into three dimensions, it should be covered with a piece of ¼- or ⅜-inch-thick foam padding. Cut out a piece of foam padding large enough to cover the entire door panel. Spray the back of the foam padding and the front of the door panel with contact cement and allow it to become tacky. Now position the foam padding on the door panel and begin pressing it into place. Start in the middle and work toward the edges, making sure that all wrinkles are pressed out of the foam. Cut off any excess foam padding at the edge of the door panel.

Now, cut out a piece of fabric (tweed or vinyl work best) large enough to cover the door panel plus an inch or two around all edges. Fold the fabric over on itself and spray the back of one half with contact cement. Spray the appropriate portion of the door panel with contact cement and allow it to become tacky. Making sure that the fabric extends past the edges, press the fabric into place on the door panel. Working outward from the middle, press out any wrinkles and make sure that the fabric makes good contact with the foam padding over the entire surface area. Spray contact cement on the back side of the remaining half of the fabric and onto the remainder of the door panel. When the contact cement becomes tacky, press the fabric into place. When you are finished with the front side of the door panel, apply contact cement to the back side of the door panel and to the back of the remaining material. Wrap the material over the edge of the door panel and press it into place. It will be necessary to cut small slits into the material when you go around corners to prevent the material from puckering. Make sure those cuts do not extend onto the front side.

## REPAINTING EXISTING DOOR PANELS

If your vehicle has plastic door panels that you wish to refurbish, you can renew or change their color. You may need to do this even if you have purchased new replacement door panels, if they don't match your interior. Most automotive paint and supply stores carry paint designed especially for plastic or vinyl door panels. Be sure to obtain the application instructions and any other necessary materials such as primer or reducer as well.

The door panels should first be washed in warm soapy water to remove dirt, grease, or other contaminants that may present adhesion problems. After cleaning the panels and allowing them to dry, you can paint them. Be sure to use the appropriate primer (if necessary) and follow the application instructions for the particular paint you are using.

## ADDITIONAL DOOR ITEMS

A few other items around the door are not necessarily upholstery items, but they are worth mentioning, simply because they are too important to let fall between the cracks if you are rebuilding/restoring a complete vehicle. These items may look to be in good shape; however, they will not look as good when accompanied by brand-new upholstery.

### Garnish moldings

Most vehicles manufactured before the 1960s used garnish moldings around the inside of the windshield, rear glass, and door windows. In addition to covering the molding or sealer that secures the glass, the garnish moldings cover the edge of the door panel or headliner. They are held in place with screws, so their removal and installation is straightforward.

From the factory, most garnish moldings are painted if they are metal or molded in the same color as the rest of the vinyl interior panels on newer vehicles. If the garnish moldings are vinyl, they can be repainted in the color of your choice using paint designed especially for use on vinyl products.

If the garnish moldings are made of metal (sheet metal, aluminum, or stainless steel are common), your choice of finishes is somewhat larger. To match the rest of the new interior, the garnish molding can be upholstered with similar material. Cut a strip of material slightly longer than the entire perimeter of the garnish molding and about 1 inch wider. Apply contact cement to the back side of the material and to the face of the garnish molding. Allow the contact cement to become tacky, then press the material into place on the face of the molding, beginning with one end of the material at the center of the top portion of the garnish molding. Smooth out wrinkles as you work your way around the molding and make sure the material extends past both edges. When you get back to where you started, you have two choices of how to finish the material: you can cut the material so that both ends are flush, or overlap the beginning by ½ inch. The risk in the first approach is that the material will shrink and leave a gap. With the latter approach, the figure of ½ inch is not an absolute. You can use whatever amount of overlap you choose, but make it consistent for all garnish moldings. After the face of the molding is covered, spray a bit more contact cement onto the back side of the material and the garnish molding. After the glue becomes tacky, press the edges of material firmly into place on the back side of the molding. Trim off all but about ¼ inch of material from the back to prevent excess material from interfering with proper fit.

Metal garnish moldings can be painted to match or complement other painted sections of the interior. Prior to painting any automobile surface, clean it with wax and grease remover. Any scratches or imperfections should be sanded out with a Scotch-Brite pad. The garnish moldings should then be cleaned again with wax and grease remover (wiped on with one cloth, then dried with a clean cloth). Apply the appropriate primer and paint following the manufacturer's directions for application, drying time, and safety requirements.

Most automotive interior paint is the same type of paint as on the exterior with the addition of a flattening agent to provide a semi-flat appearance. For late-model vehicles, an auto body and paint supply store can decipher your vehicle's paint code to give you an exact color match. For custom colors (non-OEM), ask the counter person to add some flattening agent to the paint that you purchase. This requires some trial and error to get the look you want, so try some on an inconspicuous spot and judge your results. As the flat-

# REPAINTING MOLDED VINYL DOOR PANELS

Molded vinyl is commonly found in door panels, dash panels, floor consoles, armrests, and sometimes as a protective panel on the back side of front seats. It is also found on seatbelt retractor housings, some door sill plates, and as a complete interior covering on some vehicles. Painting these items gives them a fresh look worthy of your new upholstery work.

Proper surface preparation is the key to any good paint job and a major portion of that is cleanliness. First wash the parts to be painted with warm soapy water and a small scrub brush. Rinse the pieces thoroughly with clean water, and wash and rinse again. Wipe the parts with wax and grease remover and wipe them dry with a clean cloth. Primer designed for the paint you've chosen—which must be suitable for vinyl—now can be applied and allowed to dry per the manufacturer's recommendations. After the appropriate drying time, the color coats of paint can be applied.

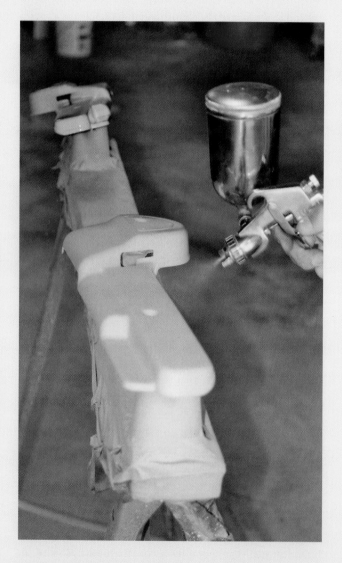

For these particular armrests, the surface is to be smooth, just like the vehicle's exterior body surfaces. To obtain this super smooth finish, the armrests are wet sanded, just like the exterior panels. Using soapy water and ultra fine sandpaper (approximately 1,000 to 2,000 grit), an upholsterer can make the armrests smooth. For an everyday driver, you may not choose to wet sand the primer as this could be considered overkill in a normal vehicle.

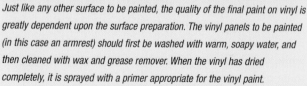

Just like any other surface to be painted, the quality of the final paint on vinyl is greatly dependent upon the surface preparation. The vinyl panels to be painted (in this case an armrest) should first be washed with warm, soapy water, and then cleaned with wax and grease remover. When the vinyl has dried completely, it is sprayed with a primer appropriate for the vinyl paint.

Since vinyl products have a certain amount of "flex" when compared to sheet metal body parts, the paint products used to cover them must be able to flex as well. If the paint is not flexible, it will most likely crack and peel off when the surface that it is applied to flexes. Most automobile paint manufacturers have their own line of products for painting vinyl trim pieces. Like exterior colors, these are available in exact color matches for factory colors as well as custom colors.

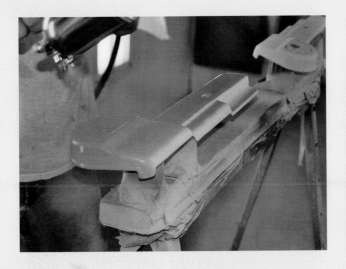

As with any automotive paint, follow the manufacturer's suggested mixing proportions, air pressure, flash time between coats, and drying times.

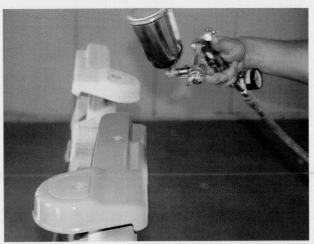

After the recommended drying time between coats, add a second coat. Be sure to apply paint from all sides to avoid areas with no paint coverage.

tening agent cannot be removed from the paint, it is better to try a small amount and then add flattener as desired.

Aluminum or stainless-steel garnish moldings or any other interior trim can be polished as well. With a Dremel or other similar rotary tool and the proper attachment and polishing compounds, you can make these metals gleam like chrome. To obtain the look of billet aluminum, aluminum trim can be scuffed with a Scotch-Brite pad and then protected with a coat or two of clear paint. Another option for aluminum trim is to have it anodized any of a variety of colors; however, this is not commonly done on garnish moldings.

### Window run channels

These are the felt-lined channels that keep the top and edges of the window glass from moving and rattling around while the vehicle is moving. If you are only performing upholstery work on your vehicle and the existing window run channels are in good shape, you don't need to replace them. However, if you are doing a complete makeover on the vehicle and repainting the doors, the window run channels should be replaced. Of course, you should make this decision and remove the channels prior to painting the doors. This allows the paint to cover this area that may or may not be completely covered by the new window run channels. Window run channel is installed by sliding one end down into the back of the door, then pressing the channel into place up, around the top of the door, and then down the front of the door. Each end of the window run channel is usually held in place by a clip built into the inside of the door. Some vehicles also secure the window run channel with additional small flathead screws.

### Window whiskers

Window whiskers are the thin pieces of trim that have whisker-like material attached to one side and are located on the interior side of the door glass. The trim is attached to the lip of the door at the base of the window opening with adhesive, small screws, or rivets. Its purpose is to keep the glass from rubbing on the door when being raised or lowered. Some vehicles have these whiskers on the exterior side of the window as well; however, a thin rubber strip to keep moisture from running into the door is more common.

### Rubber weather stripping

Whether you add insulation to your vehicle or not, it will be ineffective if the rubber weather stripping is missing or damaged. For all intents and purposes, it is impossible to make an opening automobile door that also seals completely. This makes weather stripping a necessity if you want to keep exterior climate and noise out. Weather stripping comes in a variety of cross sections for a variety of applications. Most suppliers can provide samples or drawings of what they sell to give you an idea of what to purchase.

Determine first if the weather stripping should be fitted to the door or the doorjamb. Measure around the area where the weather stripping will be applied and then order about an extra foot for each piece that you need. Clean the surface to which the weather stripping is to be applied with wax and grease remover. Apply a bead of 3M Weatherstrip Adhesive to the back side of the weather stripping and press it into place. Use some strips of masking tape approximately a foot apart all the way around the length of the weather stripping to hold it in place until the adhesive sets.

# CHAPTER 7
# CARPET

To do a good job installing carpet and optional insulation, you will need to remove the seats from the vehicle. This is not difficult and is only a little cumbersome with a large bench seat. Since you are going to the trouble to replace the carpet, you might as well remove and replace the padding and any insulation as well. An old putty knife works well to scrape up the old insulation. With the seats, old carpet, and old insulation out of the way, now is a great time to survey the condition of the floorpan as well. Installing insulation, padding, and carpet over a floorboard that is full of rust holes is a waste of money and time.

Use a mild solvent or liquid dishwashing soap and water along with a scrub brush to clean the inside of the floorpan. Any holes in the floorpan (small or large) need to be repaired if you want your new carpet to last. Ideally, any holes found in the floor would be repaired by welding in a new piece of sheet metal (or filled with the proper combination of fiberglass mat/cloth and fiberglass resin if the body is fiberglass). We have seen floors repaired by attaching a piece of sheet metal to the surrounding area by rivets. A slightly better version of that repair would include

*The carpet (like most of the rest of the interior) of this Chevrolet Beretta has seen better days and needs to be replaced if the rest of the interior were replaced. The carpet has seen a fair share of grease, grime, and mud, along with a few cigarette burns. If the seats were reupholstered and the carpet not replaced, the new interior would never look as good as it would if the carpet was replaced as well.*

the use of roofing tar between the panels to minimize moisture-related problems. Using whatever method you feel comfortable with to patch holes, now is the time to do it. Be sure to remove all rust first, or it will continue to fester.

With all holes filled, you may choose to repaint the floorpan, using a rust inhibiter. Be sure that you follow the directions, use the correct primer, and allow for the proper drying times.

## INSULATION MATERIAL

With a solid floorpan that is nice and clean, you can begin to install insulation material. For many vehicles, you can buy insulation material cut specifically for your vehicle when you purchase your new carpet. This is undoubtedly the easiest to install as it is already the correct size, or at least close. You may need to trim it some, but you shouldn't need to very much. Sometimes it will need to be trimmed only to allow for specific options such as a console or shifter.

Perhaps the best way to install this type of insulation is to fold the piece in half, front to back. The use of adhesive or double-sided tape to secure the insulation is optional, but now is the time to apply it if you are going to use it. If using contact cement, apply it to the floorpan and the back of the insulation. If using double-sided tape, apply it to the back of the insulation around the edges and in several locations toward the middle. Be sure to remove any protective strips that may be on the remaining side of tape. Position the insulation on the floor over the transmission tunnel in the front of the car, then unfold it, thus covering the rear portion of the vehicle. With some help from someone on the opposite side, push or pull the insulation as needed, so that it is centered front to back, and side to side. With the insulation in the proper position, smooth out any wrinkles or bubbles with your hands. If you have applied contact cement or double-sided tape, apply some pressure to the insulation to help the adhesive bond.

Once you are satisfied that the insulation is located properly, trim the material away from seat mounting tracks or seatbelt mounting holes. A sharp utility knife works to trim this material.

## CARPET TYPES

Most automotive carpet is either of the loop variety or a cut pile. The noticeable difference is that the carpet has loops or it has cut ends. Blended loop carpet is a combination of

*The multicolored material is jute felt insulation. Many street rods have a master cylinder located beneath the floor. Since the master cylinder may need to be filled on occasion, you need to have access to it (or a remote fill master cylinder). In this particular street rod, access to the master cylinder is gained by removing the carpet and an oversized access plate secured with four screws. The carpet in this case is designed as several overlapping pieces rather than one piece. The uppermost pieces are held in place with hook and loop material that attaches itself to the carpet below it, yet is easily pulled loose when necessary.*

materials, usually rayon and nylon. This type of carpet was used extensively in most domestic vehicles from the 1950s through the early 1970s. Cut pile carpet, usually nylon or more expensive Wilton wool, is commonly found in vehicles manufactured from the early 1970s up through the present.

## REPLACING CARPET

Most factory and aftermarket carpet is now molded carpet designed to fit a specific vehicle. This is all well and good; however, aftermarket carpet isn't available for all vehicles. Even if it was available, many people prefer the look of a hand-tailored carpet. Buying the necessary carpet and sewing it yourself also has the advantage of being less expensive than a molded one-piece replacement.

### Measuring

Begin by removing seats, scuff plates, shifter boots, and anything else that may be holding down the original carpet. The carpet can usually be peeled up with ease, as it is usually not glued into place. If it does seem difficult to remove in spots, check to be sure that it is not being held by something that needs to be removed such as a seatbelt. If the carpet appears to be stuck from underneath, slide a wide

putty knife underneath the carpet to release any glue that may have been used.

Prior to discarding the old carpet, take a look at the back side of it to see if it shows any signs of seams that may give you an idea on how to piece the new carpet together. If the existing carpet was still fitting decently (not stretched or torn), you may be able to use it as a pattern.

Now measure the floor front to back and side to side and allow about an extra 20 percent each way. Remember that the carpet typically goes up the inside of the firewall far enough that no part of the bare firewall is seen from anyone in the front seat. Accurate measurements allow you to purchase the correct amount of padding and carpet.

### Padding

All carpet should have padding beneath it, so don't scrimp and leave this out. Installing carpet without padding is simply a matter of being penny wise and pound foolish, as you will soon be replacing the carpet.

The three types of automotive carpet padding are jute felt, Polyfoam, and rebond. Jute felt is typically thought to be the best, due largely to its insulating qualities, but is the most expensive of the three. Polyfoam works well in floorpans as it can be used in compound curved areas with no crease, and is a good combination of material and price. It also has better insulating qualities than rebond. Rebond is recycled material that is environmentally sound and not quite as expensive as the other types of padding.

When using Polyfoam padding, cut a piece the desired size, push it into the floorpan, and center it front to back, and side to side. If a floor shifter and/or emergency brake lever is present, cut slits in the padding so that it can be slipped over these appendages. If a boot is used, you won't have to be quite as accurate in your cutting. A note of caution: Cut away enough of the padding so it does not restrict the movement or in any way hinder the operation of the shifter or emergency brake.

With the padding cut to the correct size and properly positioned, fold approximately half of it over on itself, and apply contact cement to both the floor and the back of the padding. When the contact cement becomes tacky, push the padding into place. Now fold the other half of the padding over and repeat the contact cement procedure.

Jute and rebond padding is thicker than Polyfoam and requires that each section of the floor be covered with a separate piece of padding. Using one piece of these types of padding would result in wrinkles. On all but the flattest of floors, one piece of padding should be cut to fit over the transmission hump, and separate pieces for each side of the floor.

## Cutting

For most vehicles, you will need to cut three pieces of carpet. The first will cover the transmission hump; the other two will cover the floor to either side. Depending on the vehicle, you may choose to add fourth and fifth pieces to cover each side in the rear seat area. If adding these two last pieces in the back, remember to position them so that any seam or overlap is beneath the front seat for aesthetic reasons.

Instead of cutting carpet right from the start, make a pattern out of Kraft or pattern paper. Roll out a piece of material that is longer and wider than the pattern needs to be. Draw a centerline on the paper that represents the centerline of the transmission hump. Now measure front to back from up under the dash to the back end of the hump and transfer this measurement to the pattern.

Where this hump meets the flat floor will be a series of straight lines on some vehicles, while on others it will be a curved line. If it is a series of straight lines, you can measure back from a reference point along the centerline of the hump and over to where the hump meets the floor at each angle point. If the meeting of the hump and the floor forms a curved line, make more measurements front to back (again from a reference point) and then measure over. Then connect the dots on your pattern until the pattern looks similar to the transmission hump. From this first line that represents where the transmission hump meets the flat floor, add a second line outward (as to make the pattern bigger) approximately 3 inches. Now cut along this outer line to form your pattern.

Check the pattern by laying it out over the transmission hump to make sure that it covers all that it is supposed to. If you have a floor shifter, locate it on the pattern as well. It will be easier and less expensive to repair the pattern than the carpet if the hole for the shifter is in the wrong place.

Now measure each side of the floor from the door over to the transmission hump. Also, measure front to back from under the dash to under the back seat where the carpet will end. Add about 3 inches in each direction. If using separate pieces in the rear, measure from the middle of the area beneath the front seat to the endpoint under the back seat. Be sure to indicate on the pattern which way is to the front and which pattern is for which side, as they are different on some vehicles.

After cutting out the patterns, lay them all out on the carpet. Situate them so that the arrows pointing to the front all point the same direction on all pieces. Carpet has a directional "nap" similar to grain in wood. You want the carpet running in the same direction. Use a piece of chalk to mark the outline of the pattern on the carpet. Use a sharp pair of shears to cut out the carpet.

## Binding

In some instances, such as anytime that more than one piece of carpet is being used, or when a rough edge is not covered by a doorsill plate or shifter boot, bind the edge of the carpet (see Figure 7-1). First measure the length of binding needed. Cut out a piece of vinyl or leather that is the necessary length and approximately 2 inches wide. Place the 2-inch wide binding material face down on the top side of the carpet and align the edges. From this common edge, measure inward ½ inch and stitch the length of the binding. Apply glue to the back side of the carpet from the edge to approximately 1½ inches from the edge. Now fold the binding material over the edge so that the carpet is covered. Press the binding in place on the back side of the carpet until the adhesive is dry. Once the glue has dried, stitch along the finished edge of the carpet through the binding on the back side of the carpet to make the binding permanent.

## Installing

Begin by positioning the center piece of carpet over the transmission hump. Center it side-to-side and make sure that the carpet goes up high enough on the inside of the firewall and far enough under the back seat to hold it in position. If you made your pattern correctly, about 3 inches of carpet will extend onto the flat portion of the floor on each side.

If you have a floor shifter, cut a small hole in the carpet so that it may slide down over the shifter. If the shifter has a removable boot, you can cut the carpet a little more to ease the installation over the shifter knob, as the raw edges can be covered by the boot. Without a removable shifter boot, make short, radial cuts in the carpet to allow the carpet to pass over the shifter. In the latter case, sew a piece of binding around the hole through which the shifter protrudes. If you do not have a floor shifter, covering the transmission hump is practically done.

Where the transmission hump turns upward to the firewall to cover the bell housing, additional work is required to obtain a good fit. Press the carpet firmly into the crease formed by the vertical portion of the firewall and the horizontal portion of the floor. At this crease, fold the upper portion of the carpet (the part that will cover the firewall) backward toward the rear of the vehicle. Cut along this crease from the bottom of the driver side to the bottom of the passenger side. Since you allowed 3 inches of overlap on either side of the transmission hump, there is still just one piece of carpet, but it now has a long slit in it (extending the width of this piece except for 3 inches on each side). Sew a piece of carpet binding to the top edge of this cut

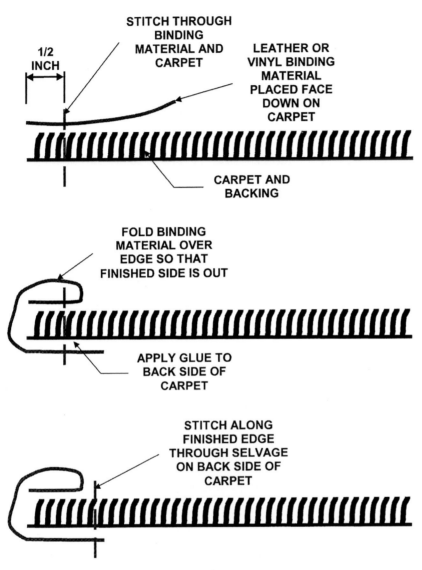

**1/2 INCH**

**STITCH THROUGH BINDING MATERIAL AND CARPET**

**LEATHER OR VINYL BINDING MATERIAL PLACED FACE DOWN ON CARPET**

**CARPET AND BACKING**

**FOLD BINDING MATERIAL OVER EDGE SO THAT FINISHED SIDE IS OUT**

**APPLY GLUE TO BACK SIDE OF CARPET**

**STITCH ALONG FINISHED EDGE THROUGH SELVAGE ON BACK SIDE OF CARPET**

NOTE: Drawing is not to scale and is merely a representation. Binding should be wrapped smoothly around the edge of the carpeting.

**Figure 7-1**

press the carpet into place. Repeat the process for the opposite side. It is not necessary to cement the top.

Now move to the passenger side carpet. Lay the carpet in place, making sure that the side of the carpet lines up with the outer edge of the floor. This edge is usually held in place by the edge of the doorsill plate, which is screwed down upon it. Trim this edge as necessary to fit properly before making any cuts on the inboard side. With the carpet positioned properly, cut the carpet in the crease where the front part of the floorpan meets the rounded portion in front of the transmission hump, and along the crease between the transmission hump and the floor. (In this case, you will cut the entire length of the crease, not leaving the ends attached as with the transmission tunnel piece.) Sew a binding edge along the front and inboard edge of the passenger side carpet. Cut out the carpet as necessary to clear the seat mounting/sliding mechanisms and seatbelt mounting holes. Secure the carpet with the doorsill plate at the doorway and by applying contact cement to the inboard half.

The driver side carpet is installed the same way; however, foot pedals may necessitate some additional work. Brake and clutch pedals that swing from under the dash pose no problem. Those that protrude through the floor, as on old VWs and Porsches and many old Amer-

from the back side of the carpet. In other words, even though we haven't fully separated the pieces on either side of the cut, consider what lies above the cut to be the "top" piece. You will sew the carpet binding to the bottom of that, from the carpet's back side. When the carpet is installed, the finished edge will cover the raw edge due to the change in direction of the carpet from horizontal to vertical.

When this portion of the carpet fits correctly, cement it in place. Fold up one side of the carpet onto itself. Spray contact cement onto the back side of the carpet and on the exposed floor. Allow the cement to become tacky, and then

ican vehicles, require more effort. Some of these pedal arms are easily removed from underneath the floor, while others have pedal pads that can be removed. Either way, cut a small slit in the carpet for each pedal. Depending on the size of the slit, you may choose to sew binding around the hole. For the throttle pedal, cut a slot for the actuator cable, or if you can remove the cable, you can cut a hole and install a grommet. You would then pass the cable through the grommet and reattach the cable to the throttle pedal. The pedal itself can usually be secured to the floor through the carpet. If you have a floor-mounted dimmer switch, it is

*Above left: The carpet in this 1932 Ford Tudor sedan is made up of several pieces that overlap slightly, rather than one piece. The rear portion of the floor is flat and has no obstructions (other than an emergency brake lever), while the front portion is required to curve over and around the transmission bell housing and fit around the steering column and brake pedal. When using multiple pieces of carpet, make sure that the nap of the carpet runs the same way and that the edges of carpet are located beneath the seats whenever possible. Above right: Most vehicles use some sort of sill plate to secure the edge of the carpet in the doorway to prevent passengers from catching their toes under the carpet and pulling it loose. OEM sill plates have been made from stainless steel, aluminum, and vinyl. No matter what the material, most are secured to the floor with two or three screws.*

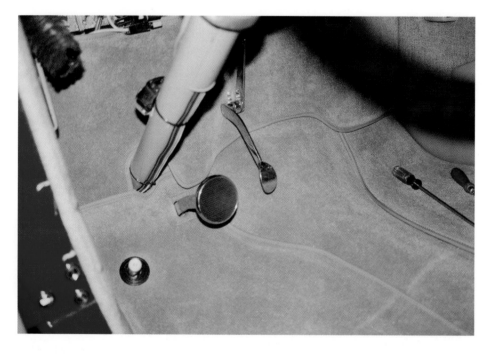

*To deal with the obstructions in the front of the interior floor, Don used several pieces of carpet to make things easier and to make the result look better. The transmission hump and tunnel is covered first and then a second piece is used for the passenger side. When the passenger side is finished, the pattern for it could be further modified for use on the driver side where all the obstructions are located. Since there are no real reference points from which to locate the steering column, dimmer switch, brake pedal, and throttle in relation to each other, an additional piece of carpet was designed to cover the area under the dash, minimizing the chance of error.*

easy enough to cut out around the round dimmer switch and then sew a binding edge to it.

Another consideration is to choose between a heel pad or to use a set of floor mats. Place a heel pad where it will provide the most protection for the carpet and then trace around it with chalk. Remove the carpet and sew the heel pad into place. Now secure the carpet into place with contact cement and the doorsill plate. Some trimmers prefer floor mats to a heel pad. Floor mats are easier to replace when necessary and easier to remove and clean until then. Floor mats can usually be made from scrap pieces of carpet, making them very inexpensive. Cut the floor mats to the desired shape and size, and finish them by sewing on a binding edge.

# CHAPTER 8
# HEADLINERS

Although a headliner never receives the wear and tear that a seat does, they are replaced often enough that some shops specialize in headliners only. Other than when completely reupholstering a vehicle, headliner replacement is usually necessary due to gravity causing it to sag. When a headliner fits like it should, it looks great, but when it pulls loose and sags, it looks real bad, real quick.

## INSULATION MATERIAL

If you are replacing the headliner, the old one will need to be removed in its entirety, so now is a great time to replace (or possibly install for the first time) some insulation material. This relatively minor step will go a long way toward keeping your vehicle more comfortable in hot weather.

Insulation can be any of a number of materials, but the most common in automobiles are jute felt and foil-backed thermal sheeting. Insulation material to be used between the headliner and the roof needs to be as lightweight as possible. After cutting the material to fit, it should be held in place with a superior-grade contact cement designed for this particular purpose (rated to withstand at least 165 degrees Fahrenheit). Since gravity will be working against you, insulation that comes loose will have great potential to cause the headliner to sag.

## TYPES OF HEADLINERS

Headliners are basically one of three types, depending on the vehicle. Older vehicles manufactured prior to World War II—before tooling was available to make the solid tops that we are accustomed to today—used structural supports to support a vinyl roof insert. These structural supports and the inside of the roof are usually covered with upholstery material stretched over top bows. This type of headliner is the most labor intensive to replace. Similar headliners are found in vehicles manufactured after World War II as well; however, the actual roof is solid in the later models. On these vehicles, the inside of the actual roof material (vinyl or sheet metal) is what you see from the passenger compartment if the headliner is not in place. This should make it apparent that damage to the roof can quickly cause damage to the interior.

The second type of headliner is no headliner at all. This is seen in lower priced vehicles and pickup trucks commonly manufactured from the 1950s through the late 1990s. Double-wall construction is what allows auto manufacturers to eliminate traditional headliners. The inside of the roof on many of these vehicles, as well as fiberglass reproductions of earlier vehicles, is usually smooth (although it may have character lines to provide support) and is painted the same color as the rest of the interior of the vehicle. Rather than painting this expanse of sheet metal or fiberglass, many builders make good use of high-quality contact cement, lots of foam, and a material such as tweed or vinyl to make sculptured headliners. These sculptured headliners are constructed in similar fashion to a door panel and are attached to the inner roof panel with self-tapping sheetmetal screws.

Most late-model vehicles have a third type of headliner: a piece or group of pieces of formed material shaped to fit the inside of the roof and covered with a variety of materials, ranging from simple to quite plush. This same technology is used to cover the door pillars and many of the other inside panels. These panels are held in place by other trim pieces, coat hooks, and passenger assist handles (also known as "oh-[expletive of your choice]" handles). Replacing this type of headliner is usually just a matter of ordering a replacement from the dealer, removing the various trim pieces that secure the headliner, removing the headliner, and holding the replacement in place while someone secures all the trim pieces that hold it.

## HEADLINER ACCESSORIES

In addition to the headliner in your vehicle, a few other items are above you that you may have forgotten about. Typically, some of them are upholstered while others are not; however, if you forget them, they may look dingy when reinstalled with your new upholstery. All these items are used to secure the headliner in place in newer vehicles that have a formed headliner.

### Sun visors

Some vehicles have an exterior sun visor located above the windshield, but in this case, the subject is the sun visor(s) located on the inside of the vehicle. These are mounted on a spring-loaded pivot near the front top of the car so that they can be used to shield your eyes from the sun coming through the front windshield or the door glass.

A typical sun visor consists of three major components: the visor mounting bracket, the visor flap, and the optional upholstery. The mounting bracket is a metal rod with a slight bend in the middle and is attached with three small screws that thread into sheet metal above the headliner. The visor flap is a piece of pressed board with a piece of metal attached to it that slides over the mounting bracket. The bend in the mounting bracket is what causes the visor flap to stay where you want it. Obviously, an unupholstered visor flap will serve its intended function just fine; however it won't look nice unless it is covered with material similar to the rest of the interior.

Sun visor mounting brackets are not universal in fit as they do differ among vehicles. Even so, a suitable replacement can often be found in similar vehicles of different makes, but from the same manufacturer, e.g., Chevrolet, Buick, Pontiac, and Oldsmobile. For this reason, if your sun visors are missing or are damaged beyond repair, you can probably find the essentials in a salvage yard. As long as you have the mounting bracket and the portion of the flap that slides over the mounting bracket, you can make your own visor flap out of particle board, Masonite, plywood, or even aluminum, as long as the material is about 3/16 inch thick.

Once you have a visor flap, you can wrap it with the material of your choice and sew the raw edges together, making this a simple project. If you want, attach some padding to the visor flap prior to wrapping it.

### Rearview mirrors

You should not forget the rearview mirror in your vehicle, as you should be using it whenever you drive. In older vehicles, the rearview mirror was usually mounted on a pedestal that hung from a mounting point just above the windshield and was held in place by two or three screws. Newer vehicles usually mount the rearview mirror on a bracket glued to the inside of the windshield. Whichever type you have, it can probably be made to look at least a little bit better by removing it from the mount and cleaning it with some good soap and water.

Depending on the color of your vehicle, the color of the housing of your rearview mirror, and the color of your new upholstery, you may choose to paint your mirror housing. This easily can be done by removing the mirror from the vehicle, cleaning it with soap and water, masking off the glass part of the mirror, then painting the housing the color of your choice. If you have recently painted your vehicle (inside or out), you probably have enough of that paint leftover to paint the mirror. A touchup gun or an airbrush works great when painting something this size, as not much paint is required. If you don't have access to a spray gun or you don't want to match the color, a spray can of a neutral color paint works fine. This might be the case if the original interior and

mirror were brown/tan and you have switched to a gray/black interior or vice versa.

### Dome lights

Other than replacing a damaged lens, chances are that you won't do too much to customize or detail a dome light or other interior lights. The lens usually just snaps into place or is secured by a couple of screws, so while you are detailing your new interior, it doesn't take much to remove the lens and clean it thoroughly. Soap and water with some help from a soft brush if the lens has any texture works wonders. If the bezel is chrome, stainless steel, or aluminum, clean it with chrome polish and a soft cloth to give it a new look.

If your vehicle does not have a dome light, prior to installing a new headliner would be a great time to add one or replace one that no longer works. Of course, if the existing light doesn't work, try replacing the bulb before you go and replace the light fixture itself. A dome light needs a wire from a power source such as the fuse panel and a method of obtaining a ground (either through a wire to a suitable ground or in the mounting of the light fixture itself). Depending on the vehicle and how it is wired, the dome light may need to be switched on manually, may be turned on with the headlight switch, or will come on whenever the doors are opened.

## HEADLINER MATERIAL

Since headliners are not being sat upon and hang from the ceiling, it would make sense that they be made of a relatively lightweight material. They are not subject to weight upon them, so they do not need to be as rugged as the seat material, although it is common to use the same material for both. Vinyl is a common choice for use as headliner material. It is durable, comes in a wide variety of colors, is relatively inexpensive, and is also relatively lightweight, when compared to Mohair or leather.

### Measuring

You will find measuring, as well as installation, easier if you remove the seats first. This allows you to position yourself anywhere inside the cabin so you can see, measure, and mark things from all available angles.

On most vehicles, the headliner is the largest single upholstered panel. You will need to measure properly, and make sure you leave enough excess material to tug on in order to stretch it tight before securing it. An untrimmed headliner for a typical American-made four-door sedan may be close to 6 or 7 feet wide. Of course, you will need to be able to stretch it front to back as well, so you will need some extra material there, too.

A curved roof will take more material than a flat roof, so on those vehicles you cannot simply measure from the front to the back of the roof. You will need to measure from the front windshield along the actual location of the headliner, back to below the rear window all the way to the package tray. Then add about 12 to 18 inches. Likewise, measure from side to side along the location of the headliner, and then add about 12 inches. Also measure the spacing between top bows. Create a diagram of the headliner in the vehicle and make it large enough that top bows and roof supports can be sketched in at their approximate location. The spacing between them may vary, so you will need to indicate this spacing on your diagram.

## Cutting

Rather than one large piece of material covering the ceiling of the vehicle, several smaller strips can be sewn together so that seams run from side to side. The material and therefore the seams are measured and cut so that they coincide with top bows that span from one side of the vehicle to the other. At each seam, a listing (a piece of muslin or cotton material that is doubled over to form a loop) is sewn to the back side of the headliner material from one side to the other. When all the pieces are sewn together to form one piece that is long enough and wide enough to cover the entire area to be covered, the material is folded in half to form a right side and left side. A small notch is cut in each end of the material at the midpoint to use as a reference point to ensure that the headliner is installed into the vehicle "square." With the seams running across the complete width of the vehicle, it would be quite noticeable if the headliner was not square with the vehicle.

## Installing

The top bows used in headliners come in a variety of styles. Most are usually no more than a quarter inch in diameter and have about a 90-degree bend at the end, but they vary in the type of end and how it attaches to the vehicle. One type may have prongs at each end, while some have a pair of prongs on one end and nothing on the opposite end. This latter type is usually designed to fit into a small clip that fits over the end of the bow on one end and has its own set of prongs. This style is probably easier to slide through the listing on the back side of the headliner. These prongs slip over screws that are threaded into the wooden framing of the vehicle or into a piece of metal attached to the inside of the vehicle specifically for this purpose. Another type of top bow has nothing on the end of it and slides into holes in the vehicle's wooden framework. Since the top bows may be of varying lengths due to the shape of the vehicle, the bows and their corresponding locations on the vehicle should be labeled prior to removing bows from an existing headliner.

Begin your headliner installation by sliding each top bow into the appropriate listing, making sure the correct end of the top bow ends up on the correct side of the headliner if the ends are different. Slide the material up away from each end of the top bow. After each top bow is inserted into the appropriate listing, move the headliner material into the inside of the vehicle with the back of the material up and the front of the headliner toward the front of the vehicle.

Some upholsterers install the bows at the front and work their way back, while others start in the middle and work forward and backward. Either method works fine, but no matter how you choose, be sure that you don't skip any top bows. You should always install the next adjacent top bow, as going back to install a skipped bow requires you to uninstall any bows that have been installed ahead of it. When all the top bows are securely positioned in place, align the notch in the front and the back of the headliner with the center of the front windshield and the back window glass (or backlight for you old-timers). Slide the headliner along the top bows as necessary to ensure that the middle of the headliner aligns with the middle of the vehicle.

The excess material of the headliner and the listings will now be bunched up at the ends of each of the top bows because they are longer than the bows. Beginning at the center top bow, make sure that the headliner is centered on the bow, and cut the listing somewhere between the end of the bow and the edge of the material. Make sure that the listing is left intact to within an inch of the end of the top bow to ensure you maintain the proper curve of the headliner as it approaches the sides of the vehicle. Pull out the wrinkles on this side of the headliner. Now repeat this process on the other side of the vehicle. Alternate from side to side, pulling out the wrinkles, and trimming away excess material a little bit at a time. Be sure to keep the headliner centered on the top bows and do not cut the headliner too short so that it won't reach down to the top of the windows. With the headliner material trimmed to the approximate size at the center bow, proceed to the next adjacent bow and repeat the trimming procedure. Remember to cut off a little bit from each side, a little at a time, rather than risk cutting off too much.

With all the wrinkles pulled out, fasten the material to the sides of the vehicle at what will become the lower edge of the headliner. There are two basic methods of securing the edges of the headliner to the vehicle. The oldest and easiest method is to attach it to a wooden or plastic tack strip. Years ago, this was done by using tacks and pushing them through the material and into the tack strip. More common now is to use a pneumatic stapler and staple the material to the tack strip, or to use contact cement and glue the material in place. Quite often, a combination of the two methods is used.

A newer procedure for securing the headliner is to use a serrated metal strip. This metal strip is secured to the inside of the vehicle with screws. The headliner material is pushed up and behind the serrated metal strip with a thin putty knife. Be sure that if you use a putty knife that it is well worn and has no sharp edges that may tear through your new headliner material. Push the material behind the serrated metal strip until it is in far enough to catch and hold on the serrations. Now move to the opposite side of the vehicle and push the material behind the serrated strip until it catches. Keep moving from side to side until all the wrinkles are pulled out of the headliner. Then trim the headliner and secure it in the front and back using the same procedures.

## MAKING A SCULPTURED HEADLINER

Many newer vehicles have abandoned the traditional headliner that is basically several strips of material sewn together to cover the inside of the roof. With the improvements that have been made in spray-on adhesives, it is easy to make a headliner that has a pattern to it without sewing anything. This pattern may be a continuation of the pattern used on the door panels or a simple geometric design.

The first step is to determine the size and shape of the area to be covered. Then use a piece of pattern paper (approximately 1/16-inch-thick tag board) to cut out a pattern the same size and shape as the area to be covered. Such items as holes for sun visors or dome lights are located on this overall pattern. The design is also sketched onto the pattern. Mark the locations for screws to attach the sculptured panel to the roof of the vehicle. This can be done with No. 8 self-tapping sheet metal screws. Use screws that are long enough to go through all the material, padding, and panel board, but not long enough to cause damage to the vehicle's roof.

The design portion is cut out from the pattern paper and laid out onto panel board. Panel board is approximately 1/8 inch thick. Some trimmers use lauan plywood or preformed ABS panels. The pattern is traced around with chalk to transfer the pattern to the panel board. Make small (approximately 1/8 inch) alignment holes in the panel board. Since the panel is made of a multi-layer pattern, the alignment holes will make sure that the pattern lines up correctly. Drill the necessary mounting holes in the panel board at this time.

The entire panel will be covered with one layer of landau foam (available in 1/4- and 3/16-inch thickness). Spray the back of the landau foam with contact adhesive and then allow it to become tacky. For contact cement to work properly, both surfaces must have the adhesive applied to them. Spray the panel board with contact adhesive and allow it to become tacky as well. Then lay the landau foam onto the panel board. Working from the middle toward the edges, use a roller to make sure there are no air bubbles.

Flip the panel board and foam over and use a razor knife to trim off the excess foam. Then use a sanding board with 80-grit sandpaper to smooth the edges of the panel board. Landau foam has a slick surface, so to provide superior adhesion for subsequent layers of foam use a sanding block with 80-grit sandpaper to slightly roughen the surface.

Now use the design pattern and cut out another piece of landau foam. Use a piece of chalk to trace the outline of the pattern onto the foam-covered panel board. Using contact cement (applied to both surfaces), place the second piece of landau foam on the panel, using the chalk marks for position. Press the foam firmly into place, making sure that positioning is correct and that bubbles are eliminated.

After all the necessary layers have been glued into place, cut out the upholstery material. Unroll the material, place the headliner panel face down upon it, and cut the material slightly oversize. Apply contact cement to the back of the material and to the panel to be covered. With the material face down on the table, position the panel upon it, making sure that excess material is present on all sides.

Now turn the panel right side up and begin pressing the material into the three-dimensional design that you created with the multi-layers of landau foam. Use a small roller, such as a wallpaper roller or a screen installation tool for intricate patterns. Start near the center of the pattern and work your way out toward the edges. Larger, flowing patterns are easier to work with than smaller, intricate designs. With the material pressed into place around all the design elements, press the flat portion into place using a large roller.

Cut off excess material. Leave about an inch to wrap around and attach to the back of the panel. Spray more glue onto the material that will wrap around to the back and onto the outer edge of the back of the panel. After the glue becomes tacky, wrap the material around the edge onto the back of the panel.

Now install the finished headliner in the vehicle by threading self-tapping screws through the panel board into the inside layer of the double wall of the roof. Reinstall the sun visors, dome lights, and passenger assist handles to secure the panel in place.

# INSTALLING A TRADITIONAL HEADLINER

To get the lowdown on installing a headliner, I checked with Don Albers to see what he had in the works. He was assisting a friend of his, Jack Waller, with a headliner in Jack's 1948 Cadillac Sedanette. The headliner in a car this size is too large for one person to attempt to install by himself. By the time I met up with Don and Jack, they had already taken the preliminary measurements and sewn together enough material to cover the inside of the roof of the car.

The basic procedure for installing the headliner is to attach it to the inside top bows located approximately in the middle of the roof, stretch it to the back and to the front, then stretch it to each side. Then, any excess material will be trimmed off. Follow along as these two old-time rodders install a new headliner.

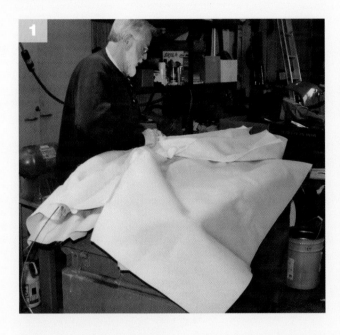

Don carefully slides the original top bows into the sleeves sewn to the top side of the headliner. Depending on the shape of the roof, some bows will be longer than others. When they are removed from the vehicle, number them so that they can be replaced in the correct locations.

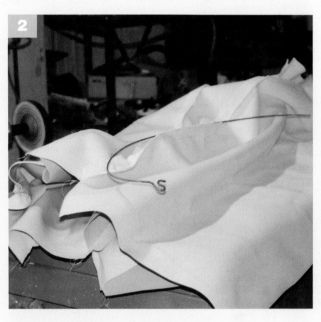

This shot gives a glimpse of what the bows look like before being installed in the headliner. For this vehicle, the top bows fit into a slotted cap on one end with a curlicue on the opposite end. The slotted end is slid through the headliner and fits over a screw head above the top edge of windows. The curlicue on the opposite ends fits over a similar screw head on the opposite side of the vehicle.

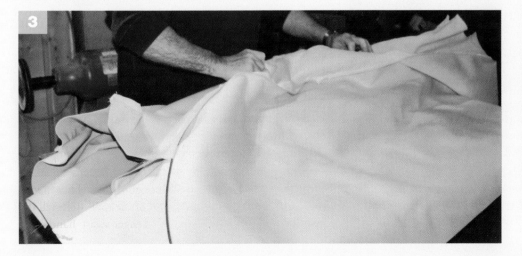

The appropriate top bow is carefully inserted into the correct sleeve of the headliner. The bow is pushed in gently from one end while the headliner material is bunched up from the other side. Continue pushing the bow in this fashion until it reaches the opposite side. Then smooth out the material and center it on the top bow.

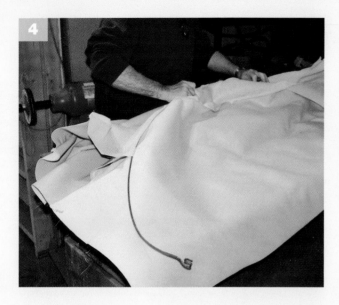

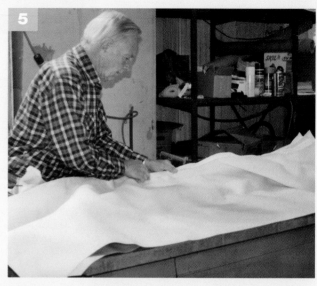

Top bows are made in a variety of styles. This style consists of a smooth round rod that slips into a cap on one end. The cap is slotted to fit over the head of a screw located just above the tops of the windows on one side of the vehicle. The opposite end of the bow is simply curled into a shape that works in the same way as the two tines of the slotted cap.

As Jack finishes installing the bows, the headliner takes some shape. It is upside down on the countertop as evidenced by the points in the material, which is where the bows are extending out of the headliner's sleeves. At this point, the headliner material is still square at the corners, but it will be trimmed later.

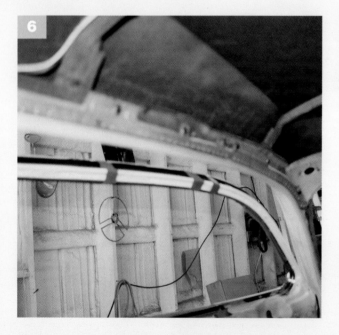

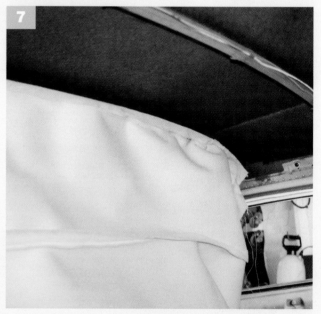

The inside of the roof prior to the headliner being installed. The inverted L-shaped piece of metal near the upper left of the photo and the metal piece that runs from about the middle of the photo toward the upper right side are roof supports; however, they also support the headliner as it passes beneath them. Several headliner bows will be positioned toward the rear of the car along with a few more between these roof supports. It's difficult to see, but the dark spots on the metal strip along the sides of the car are what the slotted ends of the headliner bows slip over.

The first bow is slipped into place, attaching to both sides of the vehicle. Obviously, the headliner needs to be right side up at this point. Some upholsterers start at one end and work backward or forward, while others begin in the middle and work both ways. As long as you get the correct top bow in the correct location (remember, they are different lengths depending on the shape of the roof), it doesn't matter where you start.

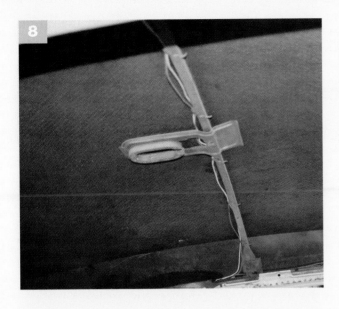

This electrical fixture is the dome light. Note that the lens has been removed so that it will cover the loose edges of material when it is reinstalled. Also note that the electrical wiring is secured to the nearest roof support and is not allowed to dangle below the line of the headliner being installed.

With the slotted end cap in position on one side of the vehicle, the top bow is raised on the opposite side so the remaining end of the headliner bow can be installed. Be sure that the headliner material is slid up on the bow so that it does not become pinched between the bow and the screw securing the bow.

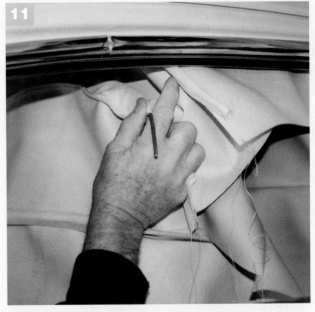

As each bow is secured in place, the remaining headliner material hangs down as seen in this photo. Depending on how large the vehicle is, it may be necessary to have someone hold the remaining headliner material up off the floor just to make sure that no one steps on it while maneuvering around the inside of the vehicle. It will be necessary for Jack to lift the headliner material up and over to install the next headliner bow. The bows must be secured in sequential order, as they are not accessible after the next one is installed.

Oops, we lost a clip somewhere in the excess material. The headliner is a curved piece in most vehicles, so don't even think that you can measure and cut the material to the exact size. For something the size of a headliner, making it even just a bit too small results in a lot of waste, so go ahead and make it plenty large and trim it to fit after it is in place.

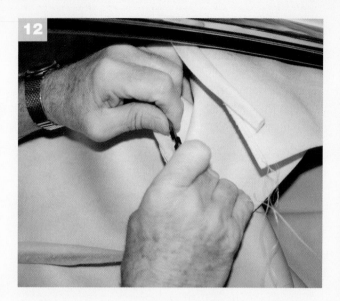

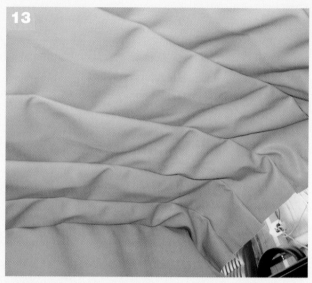

Okay, we found the clip so we can move on. A note worth repeating is that each bow of the headliner must be installed and secured correctly before moving on to the next headliner bow. Of course, if you have installed bows and must go back to another one to fix an error, it will be necessary to remove all bows in between. If you have to fix something, do so as soon as you realize the mistake.

Oh my gosh, this looks terrible. All the bows are in place in the back half of the vehicle, but still need to be installed in the front half of the car. Why does the headliner look like this? Remember all that excess that I talked about? This is normal, so don't be alarmed.

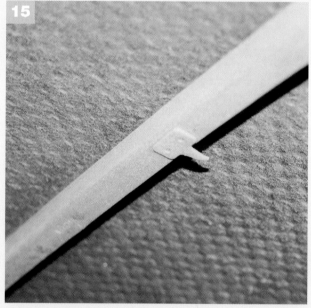

The roof support that mounts the dome light also serves as a mounting point for the headliner. The sleeve that the headliner bow passes through is attached to small tabs along the roof support.

These small tabs attached to the roof supports are pointed on the front side. The sleeves of the headliner are attached by holding the sleeve taut and pushing it over the pointed end. These serve not only to hold the headliner up, but also to help properly position it side to side as well.

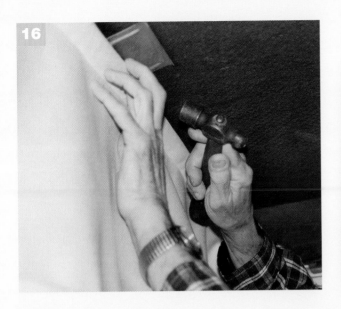

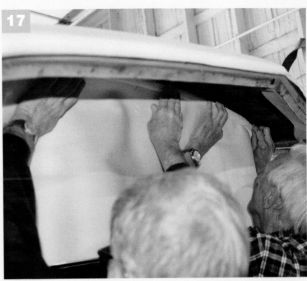

*Above left: Jack gives the small tab a few light taps with a small hammer to bend the tab upward slightly. This is done to help minimize any chance of a portion of the headliner getting caught on the tab and tearing during installation. If the tabs look to be brittle and susceptible to breakage, forego hammering on them. However, if the tabs do break (or are missing), you can make some new tabs out of sheet metal and fasten them to the roof support with a small screw or by MIG welding them into place. Note that it would be wise to assess the need for new tabs and replace them prior to getting to this point in the headliner installation. Above right: Don and Jack attach the headliner to the forward-most roof support before getting to the windshield header panel, so the majority of the headliner is in place. Oversimplifying a bit perhaps, but all that needs to be done now is pull the headliner taut, attach it to the sides, front, and back, and trim the excess.*

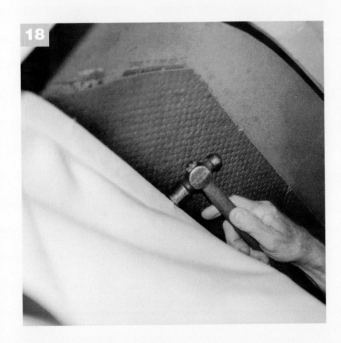

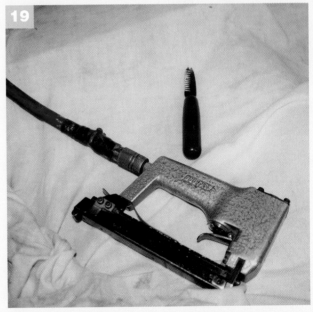

*A few taps on the tabs of the foreword-most roof support for the same reasons as on the other small tabs. To orient this photo correctly, the camera is looking upward at the roof with the light area at the upper right being through the windshield opening.*

*Two tools that are very important to this headliner installation, but are also used often throughout other automotive upholstery tasks. At the bottom is a pneumatic stapler (be sure to use the appropriate length staples for the task at hand) and at the top is a staple remover.*

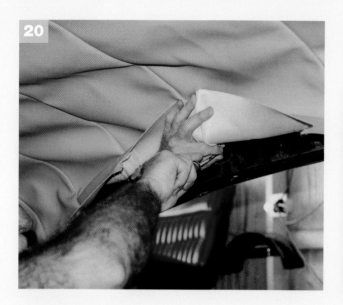

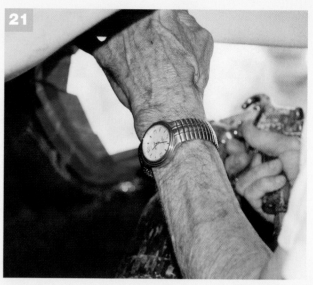

Before stapling the vinyl headliner material, Don checks to verify that all old staples have been removed and that the screws securing the headliner bows are tightened completely.

Around the rear window (backlight for all you old timers), contact cement holds the headliner in place. Jack holds the headliner material up out of the way to spray the inside of the roof around the rear window. The blue tape is around the outer edge of the window opening to protect the paint from glue overspray.

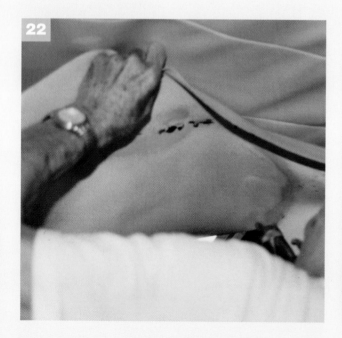

Jack sprays the back of the headliner material with contact cement. As with all contact cements, the cement is applied to both surfaces and allowed to become tacky prior to pressing the material into position. Not allowing the contact cement to become tacky ultimately will result in failure of the cement.

There may be other similar products available, but all upholsterers this author knows use 3M's Top and Trim Adhesive for most of their automotive upholstery gluing needs. It is available in various size containers and is applied with an inexpensive paint spray gun.

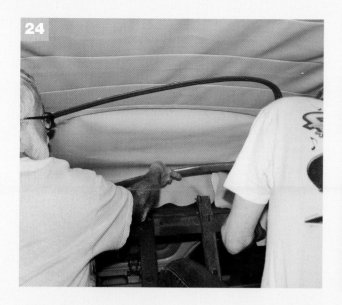

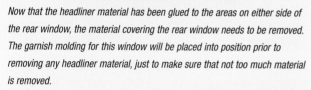

Now that the headliner material has been glued to the areas on either side of the rear window, the material covering the rear window needs to be removed. The garnish molding for this window will be placed into position prior to removing any headliner material, just to make sure that not too much material is removed.

The rear window garnish molding is held in place with several small screws. Since the vinyl will stretch somewhat and there is nothing behind the window opening, the garnish molding can be installed with the headliner material stretched across it. This ensures that the material is pushed under the garnish molding, allowing it to be stapled to the structural framework of the window.

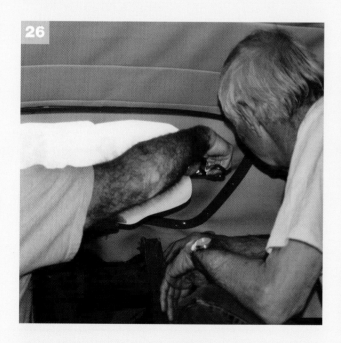

With the garnish molding in place, the majority of the headliner material can be removed. Don does this by cutting out the material with a pair of trimmer shears. Some people would be inclined to run a razor knife around the outside edge of the garnish molding to trim the window excess and use the garnish molding to hold the headliner in place. This may be necessary on some vehicles whose construction doesn't allow for the headliner to be stapled around the window opening.

This vehicle allows for the use of staples around the window opening, so some of the material is left in place so that the material can be pulled taut by one person, while another uses a pneumatic staple gun. Remove the garnish molding and begin stapling the headliner around the window opening. The staples should be spaced somewhat evenly, but they will be covered by the garnish molding, so their placement can be by eye.

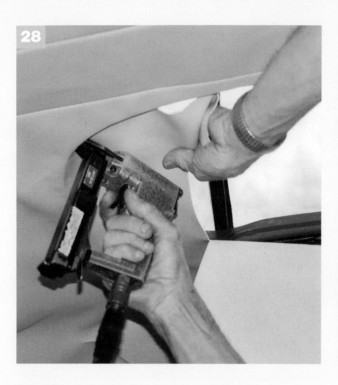

After beginning stapling at the center of the top, Jack moves to one side to work the headliner down around the side of the window and then will move to the other side.

Now that the headliner material has been stapled in place all the way around the window, the garnish molding can be reinstalled and secured with the proper hardware.

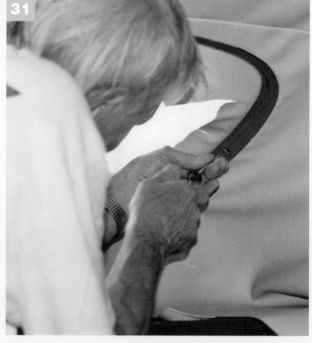

Now the rest of the excess headliner material is cut away and removed from the window area. Cut around the garnish molding with a razor knife; however, you must be sure that you do not cut into or gouge the garnish molding itself.

Jack installs the rest of the screws securing the garnish molding. Some people would just put in enough screws to secure the molding, but this practice usually results in lost screws, so go ahead and put them all in and be done with it.

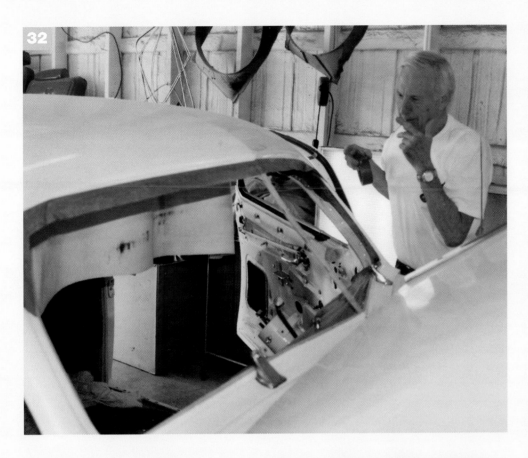

As with most vehicles when they are being reupholstered, this car has already been painted, so Jack will close the windshield area prior to spraying contact cement to secure the front of the headliner. Blue masking tape is first taped around the perimeter of the windshield opening. Then masking paper will be taped to the masking tape to prevent glue overspray from reaching the hood.

With masking paper securely in place, contact cement is sprayed on the windshield header panel and the windshield pillars. Having the windshield in place would keep glue overspray from reaching the painted exterior surfaces, but the glass would still need to be covered to protect it from glue overspray, so removing the windshield from the vehicle is probably less work in the long run.

**34**

Jack applies contact cement to the back side of the headliner material as well. Contact cement doesn't have all the bad ingredients such as isocyanates that are associated with automotive paint products, so a respirator is not necessary; however, don't be afraid to wear a mask. Anytime you spray any sort of chemical in a confined area, you are subject to some ill effects, even if temporary.

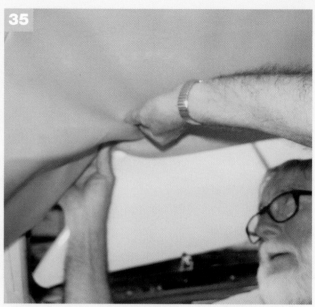

**35**

For the headliner to look nice, the material must be pulled tight. Not that you will need to bounce a quarter off it, but if the material is loose, it will look bad. The basic procedure that Don and Jack use is to hang the headliner in the middle of the vehicle, pull the headliner to the back and secure it, then pull to the front. After the headliner is secured front to back, it is pulled to each side.

Don cuts a slit in the excess of the headliner near the upper right-side corner of the windshield opening. This cut allows him to pull the headliner forward without the material bunching up in the corner of the windshield area.

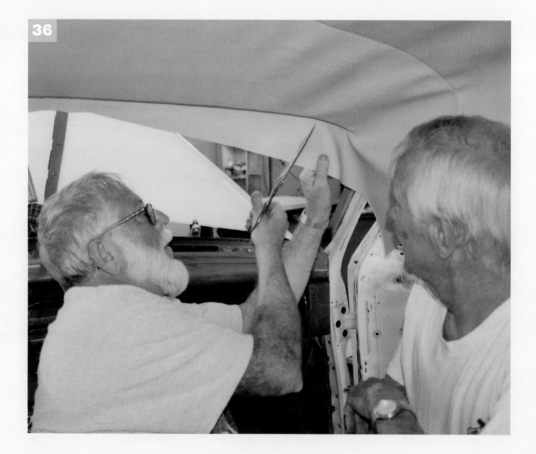

**36**

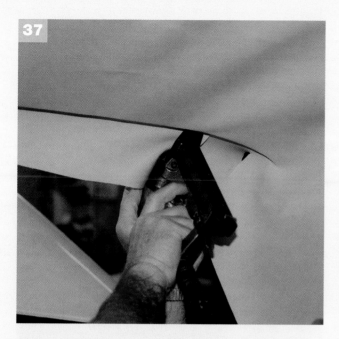

**37**

After being pulled tight, the headliner is stapled in place in the rear (inside) portion of the window opening. The windshield and its rubber weather stripping fit into place forward (outward) from this. A garnish molding covers the edge of the headliner on the inside of the vehicle.

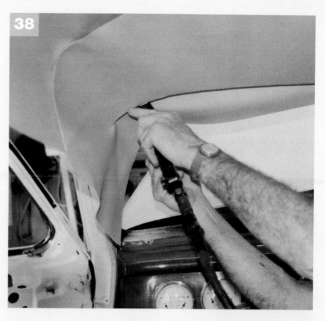

**38**

Don works his way completely across the top of the windshield opening with a pneumatic stapler. It would make sense to place some staples in the middle, some on each side, then start filling in between staples with more staples. Short of having staples on top of each other, you probably cannot put in too many.

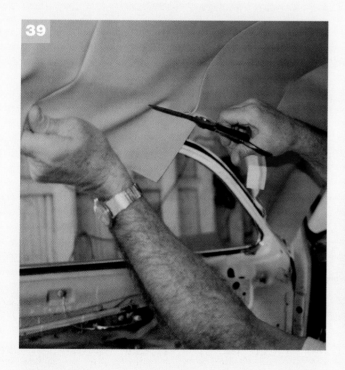

**39**

With the front and back of the headliner secured, Don begins trimming away the excess from the sides. Don't get too anxious when cutting away excess. You can always cut away more later, which is a lot easier than starting over if you cut something too short.

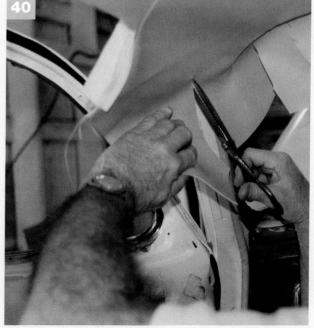

**40**

Slits in the excess allow the material to be worked around the upper left curve of the windshield in the front and the curve at the front of the door.

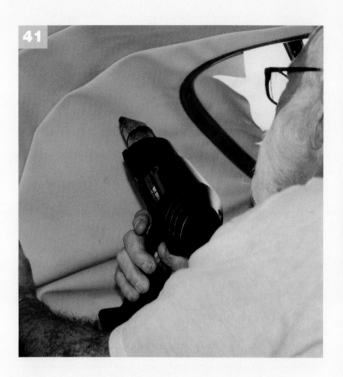

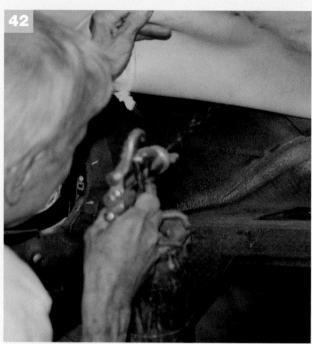

Don uses a heat gun to make the headliner material a little more pliable so it will conform to the compound curved area at the rear of the vehicle.

Contact cement is applied to the back of the headliner material and the sheet metal that forms the rear package tray. After the adhesive becomes tacky, the material can be pressed into place.

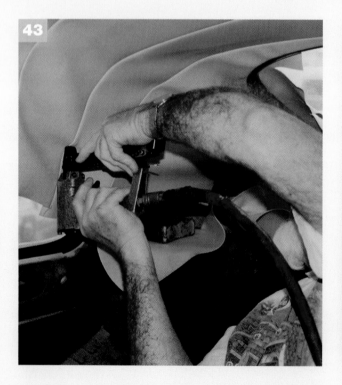

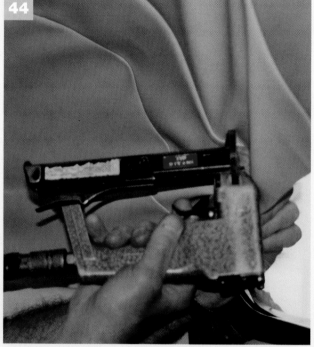

The headliner is pulled firmly but gently down to below the top of the window opening. The headliner then is stapled to the inside top of the window opening. Just like the windshield, this glass will be installed outside the headliner material, while the inside edge will be covered with a garnish molding.

The headliner is secured to the driver side window opening with staples just like the passenger side.

*The headliner is shaping up nicely in the rear portion of the vehicle. The lower edge of the headliner beneath the rear window will be covered with a package tray.*

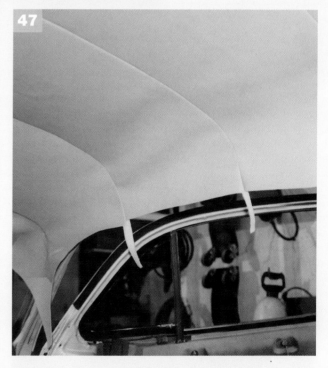

*With the headliner secured to the window opening, the excess headliner material can be trimmed away.*

*Above the door, most but not all the excess headliner material has been trimmed away. Pull strips are left in place at the headliner bows and approximately 2 inches of material is left so it can be tucked up behind serrated metal strips that hold the headliner in place above the doors.*

**HEADLINERS**

147

To push the headliner material up behind the serrated strips, Jack uses a well-worn putty knife. Using a new putty knife with sharp edges will tear the headliner material. Jack's knife has had all sharp edges and corners ground away specifically for this purpose.

The headliner material is pulled down over the smooth bottom edge of the serrated strips, then pushed upward so that the material catches on the serrated top edge.

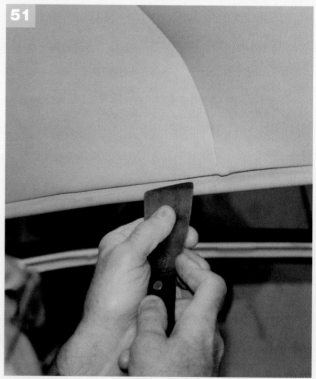

With the headliner tucked into place, Don cuts off the pull strips.

With the excess material out of the way, Don makes another pass along the door, tucking the headliner up behind the serrated strip.

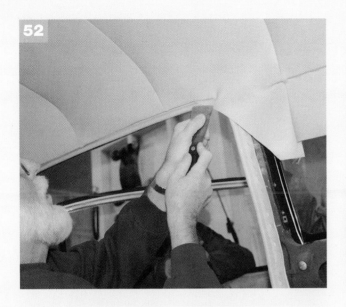

**52**

The method of securing the headliner transitions between the area above the door and the rear side window. Above the door, the material is tucked behind a serrated strip and is slightly higher than in the rear window area. To compensate for this, a section of serrated strip has been installed (prior to headliner installation) that curves downward slightly to bridge the gap between the door and the window.

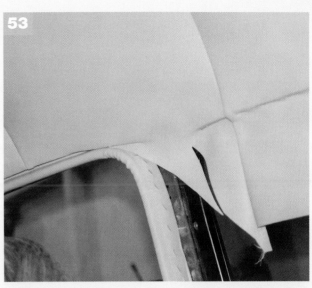

**53**

The triangular-shaped piece of headliner material still needs to be tucked up behind the serrated plate. Material behind (to the right) is stapled into the window opening and can be trimmed off. The wind lace around the door is made similar to seat piping, but uses a larger diameter cord and is stapled in place around the door.

**54**

Except for trimming in the rear side window area, this is how the finished headliner looks on the right side of the vehicle.

**55**

Excess headliner material is now trimmed away from the windshield area. Since this portion of the headliner is held in place with staples, it is necessary to use a razor knife, rather than shears to cut off the excess.

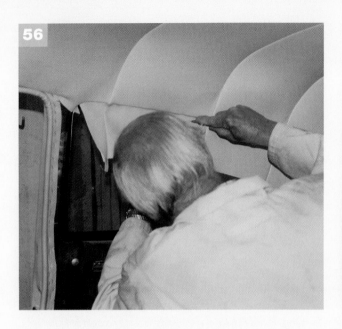

A razor knife is also used to trim the excess material away in the rear side windows where the headliner is stapled in place.

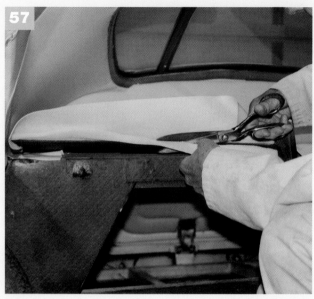

Jack cuts out a pattern that will be used to cut a piece of vinyl material that will cover the package tray. In the back, it will continue the curve of the lower edge of the rear window toward the sides of the vehicle. In the front, it will drop down over the edge that will be covered by the seat back.

The package tray material must be notched to fit around the two uprights near the middle of the seat back that serve as supports for a swing-away armrest.

To cover the package tray, the sheet metal and the back of the vinyl are both sprayed with contact cement. The vinyl is pressed into position and then held in place temporarily with lead weights until the adhesive is dry.

# CHAPTER 9
# OTHER AREAS

We have discussed most of the items in a typical automotive interior that are finished with upholstery, but there are more. In the family sedan that is getting some new seat covers, these other areas may not receive or even warrant additional attention. On a restoration or one-off custom vehicle, however, we still have a ways to go to complete the interior.

## DASH

In OEM vehicles, the dash is finished in one of three ways: fully painted, fully padded with a cover, or a combination of the two. Most vehicles built prior to the 1960s had a dash that was painted and, depending on the vehicle, decorated with various amounts of chrome or stainless-steel trim. As safety became more of an issue, manufacturers equipped vehicles with a dash that was padded and covered with vinyl. The dashes of some vehicles were completely covered, while others were padded on top and painted beneath.

If the dash is painted, you have the choice of painting it to match the exterior of the vehicle (typical on older vehicles) or using a neutral color to match the upholstered portions of the interior. On older vehicles where the color of the dash matches or complements the exterior color, the paint is usually glossy. Newer vehicles usually have a certain amount of flattening agent added to the paint to provide less gloss and cut down on potential glare, whether the paint matches the exterior or is a neutral color. Since most new paint jobs are done with a base coat that provides the color and a clear coat that provides the gloss, consider using the same base coat paint for the interior but omitting the clear coat.

Whichever color and gloss you choose to paint the dash, you typically will use the same paint for the rest of the interior surfaces that are not covered with upholstery material. If you are repainting the inside of the vehicle, remove anything and everything that can be removed from the inside. It is easier to remove a component than it is to mask it. With everything out of the way (seats, seatbelts, door handles, window riser handles, carpet, headliner, etc.), scuff the surfaces to be painted with a Scotch-Brite pad. Unless there are serious scratches or bodywork has been done, the Scotch-Brite pad should be sufficient to provide a surface with adequate adhesion for the paint to stick. After scuffing the metal surfaces, use an air hose to blow away any dust particles and clean the surface with wax and grease remover.

Prime the clean metal surface with the recommended primer and paint the color of your choice. Be sure to apply the recommended number of coats with the recommended drying time in between coats.

If the vehicle has an OEM-style dash pad, it may be faded, cracked, or peeling up from the dash. These dash pads are held in place with small screws, some of which are easy to find and some that are not as easy. Consult a collision repair manual for your vehicle if you have trouble finding all the screws or clips. Screws commonly are found on the underside of the dash along the lower front edge and up around the edge of the dash near the windshield. Remove stereo speaker grilles and defrost outlets and open the glove box door to find all the screws. Once you have removed all the screws securing the dash pad in place, it should lift right up off the dash.

Replacement dash pads are available through a variety of sources for most vehicles. Depending on the popularity of your vehicle, you may or may not be able to find the exact color dash pad that came with your car or matches the new upholstery. If this is the case, purchase paint designed for interior vinyl products from an automotive paint and supply store. Purchase the appropriate primer for the vinyl paint as well.

Wash the dash pad with warm soapy water to remove dirt, grease, or any other contaminants that may present adhesion problems. Allow the dash pad to dry thoroughly and apply the proper primer (if necessary). After the appropriate drying time for the primer, apply the color coats as directed by the instructions for the paint you are using. When the dash pad has completely dried, lay it in place on top of the dash and secure it with screws. If you have gone to the trouble and expense of reupholstering your vehicle, spend a few extra dollars and buy an interior trim screw set so that old, grungy, greasy screws don't distract from your new interior.

A dash that has previously been covered only with paint can be upholstered if the shape of the dash is somewhat uniform across its width. If the shape of the dash is inconsistent, trying to cover it with material may cause bubbles in the material. If stainless-steel or aluminum trim is used on the dash, force these bubbles to an area that will be covered with trim, and then slice the material to let the trapped air out, collapsing the bubble. After removing all the gauges, heat, and A/C controls and stereo components, remove the dash from the vehicle if possible. Remember that these openings will need to be enlarged by the thickness of the foam padding and the upholstery material prior to installing the foam padding.

Prior to covering the dash, add a layer of padding. Cut out a piece of 3/16- or 1/4-inch-thick closed-cell foam that will be big enough to cover the entire dash. Since the padding will be covered, you could splice pieces of padding if necessary. Be sure to apply plenty of contact cement near any seams and be sure to butt each piece of padding so that there is no gap, but no overlap either. Fold half the foam over on itself and spray the back side with contact cement, then spray the top half of the dash with contact cement. If you are unable to remove the dash from the vehicle and if the windshield glass is still in the vehicle, tape masking paper over the glass to protect it from adhesive overspray. When the contact cement becomes tacky, lay the foam on the dash, making sure the foam overlaps the dash in all directions. Use your fingers or a small roller to work the foam into any low spots in the dash and to press the foam firmly into place. Now spray contact cement onto the back side of the rest of the foam and the front of the dash, allow the glue to become tacky, and then finish covering the dash with foam padding. Trim off any excess padding with a razor knife. Where there are openings in the dash, use a razor knife to cut out the padding from these areas.

Upholstery material is installed in the same manner. Cut out a piece large enough to cover the entire dash, making sure to allow for some overlap around all the edges. Just as with the padding, fold half of the material over on itself. Spray the back of the material and the top half of the foam padding on the dash with contact cement. Allow the contact cement to become tacky and then press the material into place, pressing out any bubbles or wrinkles as you go. Spray contact cement onto the back of the remaining material and the front of the dash, allow it to become tacky, then smooth the rest of the material into place.

At openings in the dash, use an awl or ice pick to poke a hole in the upholstery material. If the opening is large enough, cut small slits into the material so the material can be pressed back into the opening. From the back side of the dash, spray contact cement onto the dash and the back side of the material protruding from the front of the dash. Press the tabs of material onto the back side of the dash, making sure that the edges of the openings are covered. Trim off all excess material except for about an inch all the way around the dash. Apply contact cement to this and to the back side of the dash. When the glue becomes tacky, press the material into place, covering all the edges. You may now reinstall the dash and all its components.

## Steering Column and Wheel

With all new upholstery material around it, your existing steering column and steering wheel may not look quite as good as they once did. The steering column may need some paint touchup where keys have been swinging along the ignition switch for so many miles. You could paint the steering column while it is in place; however, it would probably be less work to remove it from the vehicle than to do all the necessary masking, unless of course you are down to a bare hulk at this point already. All vehicles differ some, but the steering column will be connected to the vehicle at three locations. These are where the column passes through or under the dash, where it passes through the floor or firewall, and where it connects to the steering box or steering shafts leading thereto. A repair manual for your vehicle will offer the best advice on how to remove your steering column.

If you have decided to repaint your steering column, paint it with the same color and gloss as the rest of the painted interior components. Many custom vehicles use chrome or polished aluminum steering columns. These add some sparkle to an area that is typically plush but not shiny, making an otherwise boring item a highlight in the interior. Of course, most people spare the expense of a chrome steering column on the family sedan.

Even if you decide to keep the existing steering column (whether you repaint it or not), a new steering wheel can update the look of your interior. New steering wheels are available at automotive swap meets for around $20 to up around $400 at a variety of sources depending on your taste. Depending on the type of steering wheel you purchase and the steering column in your vehicle, it may be necessary to purchase an adaptor to make the two components work together. This adaptor is available wherever you purchase the steering wheel.

If your existing steering wheel is cracked or broken, there are epoxy kits available to repair it. If you have a perfectly restored vehicle or one that is a classic in its stock condition, repairing the steering wheel may be a better alternative than a new one. These steering wheel repair kits can be found advertised in many restoration magazines or *Hemmings Motor News*.

## Glove Box

Okay, what can you do to the glove box to make it look better? For one, take everything that isn't a pair of gloves out of it. This includes the ketchup and salt packets you pick up at the fast food restaurant, the unpaid parking tickets, the directions to that awesome party, and the ice scraper. Well, maybe you should leave the ice scraper, but clean everything else out. After you have everything out of the glove box, clean it out with a vacuum or a whiskbroom.

The actual storage portion of the glove box is made of cardboard folded and stapled into the proper shape. With the glove box emptied out, you may find that this storage container has been stretched beyond its means and is torn or otherwise damaged. While you are replacing the upholstery, you may as well put in a new glove box if the present one isn't up to snuff. They are usually not very expensive and are easy to install. Check below and inside for the relevant fasteners, as well as the wiring for the light, if so equipped. You probably noted much of this when you removed the dash pad, and if you removed the dash the glove box should be fully exposed for replacement. For popular vehicles, new glove box cardboard is available from the same retailers that provide model-specific restoration products such as seat covers and carpet kits. If not available new, search your local salvage yard for a usable replacement.

### KICK PANELS

Kick panels usually get the dirty end of the deal and are the area most likely to be forgotten about during reupholstery. Since they are located under the dash and in front of the door panels, they fall into the out-of-sight, out-of-mind category. If you have mud, dirt, or grease on your shoes or pant leg, it will end up on the kick panels in addition to the carpet or floor mats. Hard plastic or vinyl kick panels are also susceptible to being scratched, gouged, or marred by shoes or anything else that you may haul in the passenger seat. Older vehicles often have cardboard kick panels, which are easily damaged by moisture soaked up from the carpet or leaked into the window.

To inspect your kick panels thoroughly, remove them from the vehicle. They are usually held in place by two or three small screws, making their removal very easy. If they are cardboard based and are damaged by moisture, replace them. Replacement kick panels are available for many vehicles. Otherwise, they are easy to make. Begin by making a pattern of the area that you wish to cover. Be sure to include the locations for mounting holes, stereo speakers, or vents. When you have the pattern cut to the correct size and shape, transfer it to a piece of panel board or Masonite, just like when making your own door panels.

Test fit the kick panel to the door, making sure that holes for mounting screws are properly aligned. If your kick panel will have any sort of three-dimensional pattern, use reference marks to ensure proper alignment of each layer of foam padding material.

When you have the kick panel cut to the appropriate size and shaped as you wish, cover it with foam padding prior to applying the upholstery. Cut out a piece of ¼- or ⅜-inch-thick foam padding that is large enough to cover the entire kick panel. Spray the back of the foam padding and the front of the kick panel with contact cement and allow it to become tacky. Now position the foam padding on the kick panel and begin pressing it into place. Start in the middle and work toward the edges, making sure that all wrinkles are pressed out of the foam. Cut off any excess foam padding at the edge of the kick panel.

Next, cut out a piece of fabric (tweed or vinyl works best) large enough to cover the kick panel plus an inch or two around all edges. Fold the fabric over on itself and spray the back of one half with contact cement. Spray the appropriate portion of the kick panel with contact cement and allow it to become tacky. Making sure the fabric extends past the edges, press the fabric into place on the kick panel. Working outward from the middle, press out any wrinkles and make sure that the fabric makes good contact with the foam padding over the entire surface area. Now spray contact cement on the back side of the remaining half of the fabric and onto the front side of the remainder of the kick panel. When the contact cement becomes tacky, press the fabric into place. When you are finished with the front side of the kick panel, apply contact cement to the back side of the kick panel and to the back of the remaining material. Wrap the material over the edge of the kick panel and press it into place on the back side.

If your kick panels are made of plastic and are in decent condition other than being faded, they can be repainted to bring them up to the standards of your new interior. First, wash the parts to be painted with warm soapy water and a small scrub brush. These kick panels are most likely to be the filthiest pieces in the interior of your vehicle, so they may require some good scrubbing. Rinse the pieces thoroughly with clean water. If they still look dirty, go ahead and scrub them again with a new batch of soapy water. Then wipe the parts with wax and grease remover and wipe them dry with a clean cloth. Primer that is designed to be used with the paint can now be applied and allowed to dry per the manufacturer's recommendations. After the appropriate drying time, apply the color coats of paint. Be sure to follow the paint manufacturer's recommended application instructions.

### PACKAGE TRAY

The package tray is that sometimes large area above and behind the rear seat that is damaged mostly by heat from the sun being magnified as it shines through the rear window. Sometimes these package trays are made from a textured composite material that is not upholstered. Some are made of sheet metal that is painted or covered with vinyl. If the tray itself is damaged, replace it. Mounting methods vary for each vehicle, so consult a repair manual for your vehicle.

While you have the old tray out of the car or before you install a replacement, cover it with material like the rest of your newly upholstered vehicle. The slope of the back glass may make it difficult to measure for a pattern, so again, make the pattern measurements with the package tray out of the vehicle. Make a pattern from Kraft paper or lay the package tray onto a piece of ¼- or ³⁄₁₆-inch foam and cut around it with a razor knife. Then lay the package tray onto the material that you plan to cover it with. Draw a line around the package tray about an inch away from all the edges, then attach the foam padding to the package tray with contact cement. Spray the back of the upholstery material and the top side of the foam with contact cement. When the adhesive becomes tacky, position the upholstery material on the package tray so that there is overlap on all sides. Smooth out the material with your hands, and wrap the edges of the package tray with the excess material, securing it to the back with more contact cement. You can now reinstall the package tray.

The package tray, as well as the rest of the interior, will greatly benefit from tinted windows anytime that the vehicle is in direct sunlight for an extended period of time. Short of a complete car cover (which may be too much trouble for everyday commuter use), the inexpensive cardboard windshield covers designed to be placed between the windshield and the dash do help protect the inside of your vehicle while it is parked. Even if something like this is not commercially available for the rear window/package tray area of your vehicle, one could easily be made at home from thin cardboard.

## TRUNK

Two things above all others cause trunks to fall into poor condition. The first is exposure to moisture, which causes rust. The second is not as serious, but if left unattended, it will make the trunk look bad, possibly damage it and render it of little use for its intended purpose. That damaging influence is using the trunk for a storage bin, or worse yet as a trash receptacle.

Moisture commonly enters the trunk by way of worn-out weather stripping around the trunk or the back window, missing seam sealer, or through holes in the trunk floor caused by rust or collision. This moisture really causes a problem when it is trapped by a floor mat or carpet in the trunk. If you catch it before actual rust-through occurs, you can clean up and treat rust to keep it at bay. If allowed to eat through the trunk floor and spread to surrounding areas, however, rust can be difficult and expensive to repair.

Junk in the trunk can also contribute to rust by concealing and holding moisture. Corrosive agents can overturn in a cluttered trunk and create their own problems. Moreover, a junk-filled trunk isn't so useful, since you can't fit much else in there, and it's difficult to get to the jack and spare tire—which, if it's under a lot of clutter, probably has inadequate air. Now is the perfect time to reclaim your trunk and bring it to the same high standard as the upholstery in the cabin.

If you clean all the nonessential items and trash from your trunk, it will look better immediately. Instead of throwing the spare tire and jack in the trunk, stow them in their designated locations and secure them as designed. This will also probably eliminate some annoying rattles. An emergency tool kit, a first-aid kit, and safety items are acceptable in the trunk, but eliminate those empty beverage cans, snack chip bags, and anything else that is trash. Now use a heavy-duty vacuum cleaner or shop vacuum to remove the dust, dirt, and debris.

If you find any surface rust, clean it up with a wire brush. A drill attachment is a lot faster than hand brushing. With the rust removed, a couple of coats of primer, followed with a couple of coats of paint will have the trunk looking much better. If you do not have access to spray paint equipment, you can find trunk "splatter" paint in spray cans at your local auto parts store or discount store.

If the rust is severely pitted or, worse yet, goes all the way through the trunk floor, repair it by welding in a patch panel. This may require a trip to your favorite auto body shop, but ignoring the situation is not going to fix it. Since the fuel tank is likely beneath the trunk, use extreme caution in making welding repairs. The best approach is to remove the fuel tank altogether or trust the job to a professional. Whether you install the necessary patch panels or floor replacement yourself or have a professional do it, apply seam sealer to all the seams. Then prime and paint the repaired area to avoid having to make these repairs again.

OTHER AREAS

# CHAPTER 10
# UPHOLSTERY MAINTENANCE

**N**ow that you have either paid the big bucks to have your upholstery redone or have taken the time and effort to redo it yourself, you want to make sure that it lasts for a long time.

Remember that cleaning on a regular basis will take less time than waiting until the interior of your vehicle is so filthy that you cannot stand it anymore. Regular cleaning also allows the upholstery to look fresher and last longer.

The following recommendations are strictly that . . . recommendations. They are based on past personal experience—my own and others'—product claims, and advertising. You may find some products that work equally well or even better. Whatever works best for you is what I recommend—the more you like it, the more often you're likely to use it.

## CLEANING

Since vehicle interiors are usually covered with a variety of materials, no one product is best for cleaning and protecting all these freshly upholstered surfaces. Determine what kind of material needs to be cleaned and use the best product for that material.

### Fabric

Fabric surfaces include tweed, Mohair, cloth, velvet, and burlap. Due to the coarse nature of most fabrics, they are the most difficult to clean and keep clean. Use a vacuum cleaner to pull dust, dirt, and grit out of the upholstery material. Do not wipe aggressively at dust, dirt, or spilled items, as this will grind it in and may scuff up the fabric. Soak up liquids such as soda or ice cream with a dry towel, and then clean the surface with a damp towel.

### Leather and vinyl

Leather and vinyl surfaces are much easier to keep clean, making them popular materials for automotive upholstery. Vacuum accumulations of dry materials (dirt, sand, ashes) from these surfaces, while wiping away small amounts. Whether to use a dry or damp cloth to wipe away dry materials depends somewhat on the material that has been spilled onto the vinyl or leather. Many automotive detailing products are available to clean and protect leather and vinyl surfaces.

### Plastic

For cleaning most plastic surfaces, good old soap and water work well. A few squirts of liquid dishwashing detergent in a gallon bucket of warm water applied with a sponge or soft cloth cleans most plastic surfaces. For stubborn stains, squirt Simple Green or Fast Orange onto a soft cloth. It may take awhile and your elbow and shoulder may get sore before you are done, but this will usually work. If it doesn't work, consider repainting the plastic surface.

### Chrome and stainless steel

Clean chrome and stainless-steel trim with a damp cloth if they are smooth surfaces. For textured surfaces, use a soft brush to get dirt out of crevices. Substances that cannot be removed by these procedures may be removed from stainless steel with very fine steel wool. Chrome polish will usually remove the most stubborn stains from chrome.

Do not mistake chromed plastic for stainless steel as the decorative finish can be easily removed from plastic when any sort of abrasive is used. You can usually tell whether it is metal or plastic by sight or touch. If you're still not sure, try a magnet.

### Painted surfaces

Clean painted surfaces with soap and water, or with Simple Green or Fast Orange, just like plastic surfaces. Avoid using any sort of abrasive as it will scratch the paint and could eventually lead to the formation of rust.

### Carpet

Frequent vacuuming is the best way to keep carpeted areas clean. A shop vacuum is a handy accessory to have in your garage, but if you don't have one, most car washes have vacuums that cost less than a dollar per use. If you have your own shop vac, spend a few extra bucks to get one of the attachments for cleaning crevices. This makes cleaning between the seat cushion and seat back much easier, as well as between all the nooks and crannies where you can't see the stuff that accumulates.

### Glass surfaces

Fresh newspaper and a liquid glass cleaner are the best for keeping the glass clean in your vehicle. While cleaning the glass, wipe in a horizontal direction on one side and in a vertical direction on the opposite side. This helps you determine which side is streaked or spotted.

## PROTECTING

Just as a vehicle whose exterior has been treated to a good coat of wax is easier to keep clean, the same holds true for interior surfaces. Once you have the interior surfaces clean, protecting them with the appropriate products makes them easier to keep clean and protects them from potential damage when the inevitable spill does occur.

I remember as a child that it was customary for many people to purchase new seat covers whenever they purchased a new vehicle. These seat covers (often clear plastic) usually protected the seats adequately, as by the time the vehicle was traded in, the body was faded and rusty, while the seats looked brand new. In my admittedly biased opinion, it makes more sense to not cover the seats until they are no longer suitable for open exposure.

### Fabric

Scotchgard is a spray-on treatment that helps to prevent liquids and dirt from penetrating into the fabric surface. This treatment is available from some auto dealers and aftermarket dealers, but can also be purchased in aerosol cans for the do-it-yourselfer.

### Leather and vinyl

Several leather care products are available at most leading auto parts stores. Although several similar products have come along, Armor-All Protectant Wipes or spray is still what I use to keep vinyl surfaces clean. You must avoid getting this on painted surfaces or glass, however. Silicone in Armor-All products can cause adhesion problems and "fish eyes" when painted over, and it will cause some clouding on glass surfaces.

### Chrome and stainless steel

Most major auto parts or large discount stores have a multitude of chrome and stainless-steel polishes and rubbing compounds. Pick the one that most closely suits your needs and apply according to the directions.

### Painted surfaces

Just like on the exterior of your vehicle, applying paste wax to all painted surfaces on the interior is a good practice. The exception to this being any antiglare surfaces or the steering wheel.

### Carpet

Since it is usually the floor that is carpeted, and that's where our feet, shoes, boots—and whatever slush, mud, or dirt coats them—fall, carpet is the most beleaguered interior surface. For this reason, a set of floor mats is essential to keeping the carpet in your vehicle looking decent. Vinyl floor mats that can be removed from the vehicle and sprayed with a hose or scrubbed with a brush are the easiest to keep clean. Carpeted floor mats look nicer, but are in the same situation as the main carpet when it comes to keeping them clean. Their saving grace is that for the most part, they will protect the carpet beneath them and can be replaced if and when they look too bad.

# APPENDIX

**American Mustang Parts**
11315 Folsom Boulevard
Rancho Cordova, CA 95742-6208
www.american-mustang.com
800-824-6026
*Mustang restoration parts*

**Appleman Interiors**
4620 Lancaster-Kirkersville Road
Lancaster, OH 43130
740-756-4295
*Custom automotive upholstery*

**Auto Custom Carpets, Inc.**
P.O. Box 1350
Anniston, AL 36202
www.accmats.com
800-633-2358
*OEM and custom carpet*

**Bonded Logic, Inc.**
411 E. Ray Road
Chandler, AZ 85225
www.bondedlogic.com
480-812-9114
*Insulation products*

**C.A.R.S. Inc.**
1964 W. 11 Mile Road
Berkley, MI 48072
www.carsinc.com
800-521-2194
*Chevrolet restoration products*

**Cerullo**
2881 Metropolitan Place
Pomona, CA 91767
www.cerullo.com
909-392-5561
*Ready to install custom seats*

**Chevs of the 40s**
2027 B Street
Washougal, WA 98671
www.chevsofthe40s.com
800-999-2438
*Chevrolet restoration products*

**Classic Industries, Inc.**
18460 Gothard Street
Huntington Beach, CA 92648
www.classicindustries.com
800-854-1280
*Distributor of reproduction and original GM parts and accessories*

**Classtique Upholstery Supply**
P.O. Box 278
Isanti, MN 55040
www.classtique.com
866-669-6604
*Upholstery kits and supplies*

**Convertible Service**
5126 Walnut Grove Avenue
San Gabriel, CA 91776
www.convertibleparts.com
800-333-1140
*Full line of convertible parts for 1946 to present*

**Custom Auto Interiors**
18127 Marygold Avenue
Bloomington, CA 92316
www.customautointeriors.com
909-877-9342
*Upholstery supplies and interior accessories*

**Danchuk Manufacturing**
3201 S. Standard Avenue
Santa Ana, CA 92705
www.danchuk.com
800-854-6911
*Chevrolet restoration products*

**E&J Upholstery**
400 Wildwood Road
Beaufort, MO 63013
573-484-3114
*Custom automotive upholstery*

**EZ Boy Rod Interior Products**
P.O. Box 1192
Newburyport, MA 01950
www.rodinteriors.com
866-463-6439
*Seat frames, seat covers, carpet*

**Fryer's Auto Upholstery Kits**
712 NE 130th Street
Vancouver, WA 98685
www.autoupholsterykits.com
360-574-8070
*Automotive upholstery kits*

**Glide Engineering**
10662 Pullman Court
Rancho Cucamonga, CA 91730
www.glideengineering.com
800-301-3334
*Seat frames and covers*

**Goodmark Industries, Inc.**
625-E Old Norcross Road
Lawrenceville, GA 30045
www.goodmarkindustries.com
770-339-8557
*Restoration body panels and trim*

**Haartz Corp.**
87 Haywood Road
Acton, MA 01720
www.haartz.com
978-264-2651
*Convertible top and tonneau cover material*

**Harden's Muscle Car World**
P.O. Box 306
Lexington, MO 64067-0306
www.hardensmcw.com
800-633-4690
*Mopar restoration products*

**Heatshield Products**
27354 Valley Center Road
Valley Center, CA 92082-7243
www.heatshieldproducts.com
800-750-3978
*Performance heat-protection products*

**KS Reproduction Corporation**
100-A Wade Avenue
South Plainfield, NJ 07080
www.ksreproduction.com
800-599-1934
*Manufacturer of restoration and reproduction parts*

**Lebaron Bonney**
6 Chestnut Street
Amesbury, MA 01913
www.lebaronbonney.com
800-221-5408
*Ford interior upholstery, tops, and accessories*

**National Parts Depot**
900 SW 38th Avenue
Ocala, FL 34474
www.npdlink.com
352-378-2473
*Restoration and reproduction parts*

**Original Parts Group**
5252 Bolsa Avenue
Huntington Beach, CA 92649
www.originalpartsgroup.com
714-841-5363
*GM restoration parts*

**Phipps Rod & Custom Accessories, Inc.**
903 NE 42nd Street
Fort Lauderdale, FL 33334
www.phippsproducts.com
866-744-7771
*Custom interior products and custom upholstery*

**Quiet Ride Solutions**
6507 Pacific Avenue, #334
Stockton, CA 95207
www.quietride.com
209-477-4840
*Firewall insulators and AcoustiSHIELD automotive insulation and sound dampening products*

**Restoration Specialties & Supply**
P.O. Box 328
Windber, PA 15963
www.restorationspecialties.com
814-467-9842
*Upholstery supplies*

**RW and Able, Inc.**
P.O. Box 2160
Chico, CA 95927
www.roddoors.com
530-896-1513
*Door panels, seats, and interior products*

**Sam Wright Hot Rod Interiors**
304 East 1400 Road
Baldwin City, KS 66006
785-594-7430
*Custom automotive upholstery*

**Sewfine Products, Inc.**
5119 S. Windermere Street
Littleton, CO 80120-1024
www.sewfineproducts.com
303-347-0212
*Volkswagen and hot rod interiors*

**Sid Chavers Company**
880 Aldo Avenue
Santa Clara, CA 95054
www.sidchaverscompany.com
408-980-9081
*Custom upholstery*

**Street Rod Interiors**
6121 Midway Road
Ft. Worth, TX 76117
www.larrydennis.com
800-772-7542
*Upholstery tools and supplies*

**Tea's Design, Inc.**
2038 15th Street NW
Rochester, MN 55901
www.teasdesign.com
800-791-7228
*Ready to install bench, bucket, or split bench seats*

**The Glass House**
446 W. Arrow Highway, #4
San Dimas, CA 91773
www.theglasshouse1.com
909-592-1078
*windshield glass, weather stripping, and other glass-related items*

**Trim Parts**
2175 Deerfield Road
Lebanon, OH 45036
www.trimparts.com
513-934-0815
*Custom molded carpets and interior trim*

**Wise Guys**
P.O. Box 211,
Elkhart, IN 46515
www.wiseguys-seats.com
574-848-1309
*Seat frames and accessories*

# INDEX

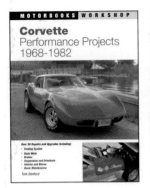
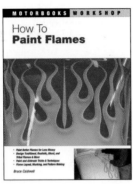

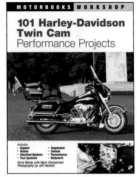